THE
McSWEENEY'S
BOOK OF
POETS
PICKING
POETS

M^CSWEENEY'S BOOKS
SAN FRANCISCO

For more information about McSweeney's, see www.mcsweeneys.net

ISBN-13: 978-1-932416-81-7

Printed in Canada

ABOUT THIS BOOK

Poetry is a notoriously subjective affair, and the evaluation of it is notoriously unstable. That's why we tried to stay entirely out of the way, letting the poems in this book pick themselves. The project worked like this: First, we chose one poem each from ten different poets. Then we asked each poet to choose another of their poems—new or previously published, we left it up to them—and a poem from another poet. That new poet then picked one of their own and another poet, and so on. Each chain was to be five poets long. The result: ten chains, five poets per chain, two poems per poet—one almighty collection of verse.

What you hold in your hands now is one hundred favorite works of some of the most vital poets writing today. As a group, little can be said about them. It's an eclectic gathering, reflecting, we hope, the variegated landscape of contemporary poetry. Yet despite the diversity, each chain has its own distinct tone. In some, common themes emerge and develop from one poet to the next. In others, we're left to retrace how the chain leapt from a poem of one flavor or hue to, a few links later, a piece adhering to an entirely dissimilar aesthetic. The connections between poets— their sources of influence and inspiration—are not always visible from the surface, and the chains do not follow predictable paths.

If the last time you picked up a poem, you were punished for doing so by being assigned a 5-7-page paper—that is, if you found yourself victim to those who think poetry is an estranged kin of, say, logic, as opposed to evidence of a heightened engagement with life, created for the purpose of dilating one's consciousness and, finally, for enjoyment— please, have no fear. There will be no assignments here. And not a single poem included mentions any Yawning Abyss, fathomable or un-.

The poems within do, however, discuss sea leopards, dogs without ethos, and a truly remarkable radish. There's also a reference to "two loaves of bread," which one of our editors thought was hilarious. (He wept bitterly, however, at mention of "an old biscuit.") We can't take any credit, but we're thrilled with how the collection turned out.

—Dominic Luxford, curator

CONTENTS

INTRODUCTION

by DAVID ORR

If you want to learn to play guitar, the process is relatively straightforward. You'll practice, get frustrated, practice some more, learn a few songs, finally pick somebody up at a party by playing "Blackbird," practice again (now with more enthusiasm), and then at last, if you're a certain kind of person, post a clip of yourself ripping through "Crazy Train" on YouTube, so that kids in the Philippines can admire the extent to which "U rawk!!!!" Your path to six-string competence may not be easy, but it won't be crooked either.

The same, unfortunately, can't be said for learning about poetry. Writing—or reading—poetry isn't exactly a skill (like mastering C#), nor is it entirely a matter of intuition (like, say, navigating a dinner party). So in trying to explain poetry to a lay audience, even the most flexible and imaginative teacher usually ends up struggling to balance two very different approaches. The first of these is what you might call the systematic method (or if you're feeling uncharitable, the boring method). As T.S. Eliot puts it in "Tradition and the Individual Talent," this way of looking at poetry focuses on the development of a historical sensibility that must be "obtained with great labor"; as you might expect, then, a teacher who favors systematic instruction typically stresses the mastery of poetry's traditional building blocks—the sonnet, the ode and so forth—and refuses to let you skip the snoozy parts of *Paradise Lost*. At its best, this method can produce a writer or reader who is wise and humble; at its worst, it produces one who won't shut up about dactylic hexameter.

The second approach—call it the improvisational method— is pretty nearly the opposite of the first. The spirit of this method is best expressed by Philip Larkin in an interview with the *Paris Review* from 1982:

> **Interviewer:** *You mention Auden, Thomas, Yeats and Hardy ... What in particular did you learn from your study of those four?*
>
> **Larkin:** Oh, for Christ's sake, one doesn't *study* poets! You *read* them, and think, That's marvelous, how is it done, could I do it? and that's how you learn.

When we think about poetry improvisationally, we're being casual, reading rather than studying, taking things as they come and making whatever use of them we can. We're relying on impulses and best guesses. This is the method Robert Frost had in mind when he claimed that he wanted only to teach "minor writers" and that he'd let his students "read what they wish. And then we'll have some fun in their telling me why they made their choice; why a thing called to them."

Poetry anthologies are usually organized systematically, but read improvisationally. Or to put it another way, an anthologist is typically obligated to be "fair"—he has to cover the ground laid out for him by a contemporary consensus, and the resulting book tends to be comprehensive, judicious, and kind of bland. Readers, however, are notoriously *un*fair to anthologies—they skip around, get bored, spill Fritos crumbs on page 15, and read some poems fifty times and others not even once. The anthologist's painstaking deliberations (How many pages for Ashbery? How many for Kay Ryan?) are breezily overthrown by his audience's desire for more short poems with dogs in them.

This book, though, is different. You can feel perfectly justified in reading this anthology improvisationally, because it was put together exactly the same way. The one hundred poems and ten different chains of association here are unsystematic, injudicious, frequently delightful, and occasionally confusing—less like a dinner party than a spontaneous sit-down.

So what do we get when we allow poets to choose their own tablemates? Some geographic diversity, for one thing. The American poet Lynn Emanuel, author of the cleverly literary "My Subjectivity," selects Tomaž Šalamun, who is Croatian. Lisa Robertson, a Canadian, picks Caroline Bergvall, who lives in London. We also get intriguing shifts from older, more accomplished writers to poets who are just beginning their careers— and vice versa. Yusef Komunyakaa, the Pulitzer Prize–winning author of over ten books, chooses a poem by his Princeton colleague Tracy K. Smith, whose second collection, *Duende,* has only recently appeared. The chain begun by David Berman (who's published one book, *Actual Air*) ends with Charles Simic, a member of the American Academy of Arts and Letters and a former Chancellor of the Academy of American Poets.

And of course, more than anything else, this anthology allows us to discover what a poet finds best in her own work alongside what she finds appealing in someone else's. For instance, Kay Ryan's selection of "Dog Leg" shows that she understands what makes her own poetry so vivid—the poem is wry, spiky with a submerged pathos, and spins along on carefully-placed rhymes with quirky efficiency. At first, it might seem odd that a poet who favors such short, narrow structures would pick a poem like Sarah Lindsay's capacious and relaxed "Cheese Penguin." But however dissimilar their favorite forms may be, the two poets have compatible viewpoints; both understand the humor and the sadness that comes, as Lindsay puts it, from knowing that "the world is large,/ and without a fuss has absorbed stranger things than this" (the "this" in question being the birth of a penguin from a cheese tin, which is pretty strange indeed).

So take a look inside; see what strange things you may find among the writers gathered here. You can skip around, you can read each chain in order, or you can read the whole book backward while making soup. Any way you choose to do it, you'll probably find something worth listening to, someone worth talking back to, somebody you'll want to have a conversation with.

1

DAVID BERMAN

↓

BRETT EUGENE RALPH

↓

BERND SAUERMANN

↓

JAMES TATE

↓

CHARLES SIMIC

THE CHARM OF 5:30
David Berman

It's too nice a day to read a novel set in England.

We're within inches of the perfect distance from the sun,
the sky is blueberries and cream,
and the wind is as warm as air from a tire.
Even the headstones in the graveyard
        seem to stand up and say "Hello! My name is..."

It's enough to be sitting here on my porch,
thinking about Kermit Roosevelt,
following the course of an ant,
or walking out into the yard with a cordless phone
        to find out she is going to be there tonight.

On a day like today, what looks like bad news in the distance
turns out to be something on my contact, carports and white
courtesy phones are spontaneously reappreciated
        and random "okay"s ring through the backyards.

This morning I discovered the red tints in cola
        when I held a glass of it up to the light
and found an expensive flashlight in the pocket of a winter coat
        I was packing away for the summer.

It all reminds me of that moment when you take off your sunglasses
after a long drive and realize it's earlier
and lighter out than you had accounted for.

You know what I'm taking about,

and that's the kind of fellowship that's taking place in town, out in
the public spaces. You won't overhear anyone using the words
"dramaturgy" or "state inspection" today. We're too busy
getting along.

It occurs to me that the laws are in the regions and the regions are
in the laws, and it feels good to say this, something that I'm almost
sure is true, outside under the sun.

Then to say it again, around friends, in the resonant voices of a
nineteenth-century senator, just for a lark.

There's a shy looking fellow on the courthouse steps, holding up a
placard that says "But, I kinda liked Reagan." His head turns slowly
as a beautiful girl walks by, holding a refrigerated bottle up against
her flushed cheek.

She smiles at me and I allow myself to imagine her walking into
town to buy lotion at a brick pharmacy.
When she gets home she'll apply it with great lingering care before
moving into her parlor to play 78 records and drink gin-and-tonics
beside her homemade altar to James Madison.

In a town of this size, it's certainly possible that I'll be invited over
one night.

In fact I'll bet you something.

Somewhere in the future I am remembering today. I'll bet you
I'm remembering how I walked into the park at five thirty,
my favorite time of day, and how I found two cold pitchers
of just poured beer, sitting there on the bench.

I am remembering how my friend Chip showed up
with a catcher's mask hanging from his belt and how I said

great to see you, sit down, have a beer, how are you,
and how he turned to me with the sunset reflecting off his contacts
and said, wonderful, how are you.

NOW II
David Berman

I am not in the parlor of a federal brownstone.
I am not a cub scout seduced by Iron Maiden's mirror worlds.

I'm on a floor unrecognized by the elevator,
    fucked beyond understanding
    like a hacked up police tree
on the outskirts of town.

Father, why does this night
last longer than any other night?

For God is not a secret.

And the brown girl who reads the Bible by the pool
with a bookmark that says "ed called"
or "ed call ed," must know that turtles
are screwed in the snow

and that everything strains to be inevitable
even as it's being killed forever.

And this is also a song.

O I've lied to you so much I can no longer trust you.

Why must we suffer this expensive silence,

aren't we meant to crest in a fury more distinguished?

Because there is my life and there is our life
    (which I know to be Your life).

Dear Lord, whom I love so much,
    I don't think I can change anymore.

I have burned all my forces at the edge of the city.
I am all dressed up to go away,

and I'm asking You now
    if You'd take me as I am.

For God is not a secret,

and this also is a song.

FLOWERING JUDAS
Brett Eugene Ralph

Every time I open my eyes
The phantoms all expire
They could be klansmen, they could be little girls
Wearing wedding dresses

Two shadows
Mine and the cat's
Stalk the summer grasses

For turtles, dewsoftened
Concert tickets, news of
Thomas Merton

Two nights they were digging
Up against the fence
In the morning the shovels
Were put away

They covered the hole with an old
Canvas lawnchair
Weighed down at the corners with cinder blocks

Weeds grown up so high now we'll never know
But there, long before the chair
Merle said they was some flowers

          *   *   *

Back on the porch
A breeze lolls
Yard to yard

Pine whisper
Thin branches only

A mourning dove emerges

Far off
The way a train sounds
The way a dog barks at night
At nobody
The way phones ring over & over when you
Almost want to answer

When it's not your phone
But you can hear it

FIRM AGAINST THE PATTERN
Brett Eugene Ralph

When I saw Charity dancing
alone in the farmhouse kitchen,
eyes closed, lips parted, held aloft
in one hand half a mango,
a gigantic butcher knife
clutched in the other—I froze
at the screen door as I always do
when I come upon someone praying.

All night I had been hitting
on the daughter of a tiny woman
orphaned by Hiroshima.
Grandparents had been lost, and her mother
would soon be dead though no one knew
if it was the blast or the facility
she retired next to in Utah.

This was the kind of bitter irony
that made you want to burn the flag—
even if it was against the law, even
on the Fourth of July on property owned
by a Republican state senator.
Which is precisely what would happen
later, after we'd drunk the wine.

Hey, he said in one of those voices
unique to fraternity members

high on nitrous oxide, *Anybody want a drink*
of hundred-year-old Romanian wine?
Before we could answer, he had produced
from one of the pockets on his wheel chair
wine he meted out, so help me God,
from a Mrs. Butterworth's bottle.

By the time that bottle made its way
around the bonfire, I was drunk
on kimonos wed to atom bombs
and motherless children left to cultivate
an excruciating beauty,
drunk on crippled tipplers
scarcely larger than dolls.
On an evening such as this, one swig
makes little difference.

Like the wine my father fashioned
out of blackberries, out of plums,
it was very sweet and very strong
and it wouldn't have taken much to turn
Mrs. Butterworth upside down
until her skirts fell and I'd forgotten
that the cloud above Nagasaki rhymes
with the flag we raised on the moon.

As I watched Charity, I rested
my brow against the rusty screen
and that knife and mango might have been
a bottle and a beating heart,

a bomb and a burned up baby doll,
a flag and whatever comes to mind
when you read the word *forgiveness.*

Closing my eyes, I extended my tongue
and pressed it firm against the pattern:
I tasted yesterday's rain, the forgotten
carcasses of moths,
broken glances, rebel tears,
the smoke of not-so-distant fires,
all those delicate gestures
we collect and call the seasons.

ARIZONA
BERND SAUERMANN

I think to rebuild all her ghost towns in silver.
I think to replicate her pit mines, which are so deep and lovely in
      the morning.
I think to relive her every daybreak as my satellites sink back into
      their orbits.

All this as a TV is turned on
and a landscape burns with spires
and the shadow of a cloud crosses the arroyo like a scar.
Then I shoot up the ceilings and walls.
Then I snake through fragrant canyons of sage.
Then I cut the pinkish ribbon of sky
and meander off into the chaparral.

Now I gesture like drifting sand.
Now I nail up the wanted posters alone.
Now lumps of lead find me,
and copper mined from the belly of my star
gets drawn into coils of regret.
Tawdry news slithers the length of my wire,
and woman, how I strip-mine the girly veins of ore from my skull
and leave a hole where each morning a mountain rose,
aflame.

SUBTRACTION FOREVER
Bernd Sauermann

Remove the bed of rolled-up rugs
in a basement room
where there are bars on the window,
and take back the gifts we gave each other:
luggage, a life-raft, and dark bicycles
standing in the corner.
Brush the lint from our backs,
and what remains is the difference between you
and deer sleeping in meadows of gentle breathing.

On the drive home, your words,
like gloomy moths, their wings
spanning the horizons of the known world,
conjured with the sullen certainty of dust,
a spell the size of that world
to take me down with them.
Desires hovered and were lost
between a dance toward oncoming lights,
a faint tick and a smear on the windshield.
A deer moved nearer the road.

DISTANCE FROM LOVED ONES
James Tate

After her husband died, Zita decided to get the face-lift she had always wanted. Halfway through the operation her blood pressure started to drop, and they had to stop. When Zita tried to fasten her seat belt for her sad drive home, she threw out her shoulder. Back at the hospital the doctor examined her and found cancer run rampant throughout her shoulder and arm and elsewhere. Radiation followed. And, now, Zita just sits there in her beauty parlor, bald, crying and crying.

My mother tells me all this on the phone, and I say: Mother, who is Zita?

And my mother says, I am Zita. All my life I have been Zita, bald and crying. And you, my son, who should have known me best, thought I was nothing but your mother.

But, Mother, I say, I am dying....

THE RADISH
James Tate

I was holding this really exemplary radish in my hand.
I was admiring its shape and size and color. I was imagining
its zesty, biting taste. And when I listened, I even thought
I could hear it singing. It was unlike anything I had ever
heard, perhaps an Oriental woman from a remote mountain village
singing to her rabbit. She's hiding in a cave, and night has
fallen. Her parents had decided to sell her to the evil prince.
And he and his thousand soldiers were searching for her everywhere.
She trembled in the cold and held the rabbit to her cheek. She
whispered the song in a high, thin voice, like a reed swaying
by itself on a bank above a river. The rabbit's large, brown ears
stood straight up, not wanting to miss a word. Then I dropped
the radish into my basket and moved on down the aisle. The store
was exceptionally crowded, due to the upcoming holiday. My cart
jostled with the others. Sometimes it pretended we were in a cock-
fight, a little cut here, some bleeding. Now the advantage is mine.
I jump up and spur the old lady, who's weak and ready to fall.
I spot a mushroom I really want. It's within reach. You could
search all day and never find a mushroom like that. I could smell
it sizzling in butter and garlic. I could taste it garnishing my
steak. Suddenly, my cart is rammed and I'm reeling for my balance.
I can't even see who the enemy is. Then I'm hit again and I'm
sprawling up against the potatoes. I've been separated from my
cart. I look around desperately. "Have you seen my cart?" I ask
a man dressed in lederhosen and an alpine hat. "I myself have
misplaced my mother's ashes. How could I know anything about your
cart?" he said. "I'm sorry to hear about your mother," I said.
"Was it sudden, or was it a long, slow, agonizing death, where

you considered killing her yourself just to put her out of her pain?"
"Is that your cart with the radish in it?" he said. "Oh, yes,
thank you, thank you a thousand times over, I can't thank you
enough," I said. "Schmuck," he said. The mushroom of my dreams,
of course, was long gone, and the others looked sickly, like they
were meant to kill you, so I forged on past the kohlrabi and
parsnips. I hesitated at the okra. A flood of fond memories
overcame me. I remembered Tanya and her tiny okra, so firm and
tasty, one Christmas long ago. There was a fire in the fireplace
and candlelight, music, and the crunch, crunch, crunch of the okra.
I have never been able to touch okra since that sacred day.
We were in the Klondike, or so it seemed to me then. Tanya had
a big dog, and it ate the roast, and we had a big laugh, but now
I don't think it's funny. I remember the smell of that roast,
as if it were cooking this very minute, and I can see Tanya
bending over to check on it. How did we ever get out of there
alive? And what happened to Tanya? I look around, peaches and
plums. I'm butted from behind. "Watch it," I say to no one in
particular. Eight eyes are glaring at me. "I'm moving," I say.
But I can't move. The rabbit says, "Tonight we will meet our
death, but it will be beautiful and we will be brave and not
afraid. You will sing to me and I will close my eyes and dream
of a garden where we will play under the starlight, and that's
where the story ends, with me munching a radish and you laughing."
"I can't move," I said.

THE DEVILS
Charles Simic

You were a "victim of semiromantic anarchism
In its most irrational form."
I was "ill at ease in an ambiguous world

Deserted by Providence." We drank gin
And made love in the afternoon. The neighbors'
TV's were tuned to soap operas.

The unhappy couples spoke little.
There were interminable pauses.
Soft organ music. Someone coughing.

"It's like Strindberg's *Dream Play*," you said.
"What is?" I asked and got no reply.
I was watching a spider on the ceiling.

It was the kind St. Veronica ate in her martyrdom.
"That woman subsisted on spiders only,"
I told the janitor when he came to fix the faucet.

He wore dirty overalls and a derby hat.
Once he had been an inmate of a notorious state institution.
"I'm no longer Jesus," he informed us happily.

He believed only in devils now.
"This building is full of them," he confided.
One could see their horns and tails

If one caught them in their baths.
"He's got Dark Ages on his brain," you said.
"Who does?" I asked and got no reply.

The spider had the beginnings of a web
Over our heads. The world was quiet
Except when one of us took a sip of gin.

THAT LITTLE SOMETHING
Charles Simic

The likelihood of ever finding is small.
It's like being accosted by a woman
And asked to help her look for a pearl
She lost right here in the street.

She could be making it all up,
Even her tears, you say to yourself
As you search under your feet,
Thinking, not in a million years...

It's one of those summer afternoons
When one needs a good excuse
To step out of a cool shade.
In the meantime, what ever became of her?

And why, years later, do you still,
Off and on, cast your eyes to the ground
As you hurry to some appointment
Where you are now certain to arrive late.

2

MARK DOTY
↓
BRENDA SHAUGHNESSY
↓
OLENA KALYTIAK DAVIS
↓
ALICE NOTLEY
↓
JOHN ASHBERY

HAIR
Mark Doty

In a scene in the film
shot at Bergen-Belsen days after
the liberation of the camp
a woman brushes her hair.

Though her gesture is effortless
it seems also for the first time,
as if she has just remembered
that she has long hair,

that it is a pleasure
to brush, and that pleasure
is possible. And the mirror
beside which the camera must be rolling,

the combing out and tying back
of the hair, all possible.
She wears a new black sweater
the relief workers have brought,

clothes to replace the body's
visible hungers. Perhaps
she is a little shy of the camera,
or else she is distracted

by the new wool and plain wonder
of the hairbrush, because

on her face is a sort of dulled,
dreamy look, as if the part

of herself that recognizes
the simple familiar good of brushing
is floating back into her,
the way the spiritualists say

the etheric body returns to us
when we wake from sleep's long travel.
With each stroke she restores
something of herself, and one

at a time the arms and hands
and face remember, the scalp
remembers that her hair
is a part of her, her own.

THEORY OF BEAUTY (TONY)
Mark Doty

Somebody who worked in the jailhouse kitchen
cooked up some grease, burnt it black, scraped the carbon
from the griddle. Somebody else made a needle
from the shaft of a filched Bic, ballpoint replaced

with a staple beaten flat, and then the men received,
one at a time, heads of Christ looking up through

streams of blood from his thorny crown, or death's heads
looming over x's of bones. But Tony chose,
for his left shoulder, the sign language glyph for Love,
a simple shape, though hard to read; he had to tell me

what it meant. And then what seemed indifferently made,
not even a sketch, became a kind of blazon,

one that both lifted and exposed the man who wore it,
as he sat fumbling with a lighter, too stoned to fire
the pipe he held, using it to point to the character
on his arm, making plain the art of what was written there.

I'M OVER THE MOON
Brenda Shaughnessy

I don't like what the moon is supposed to do.
Confuse me, ovulate me,

spoon-feed me longing. A kind of ancient
date-rape drug. So I'll howl at you, moon,

I'm angry. I'll take back the night. Using me to
swoon at your questionable light,

you had me chasing you,
the world's worst lover, over and over

hoping for a mirror, a whisper, insight.
But you disappear for nights on end

with all my erotic mysteries
and my entire unconscious mind.

How long do I try to get water from a stone?
It's like having a bad boyfriend in a good band.

Better off alone. I'm going to write hard
and fast into you moon, face-fucking.

Something you wouldn't understand.
You with no swampy sexual

promise but what we glue onto you.
That's not real. You have no begging

cunt. No panties ripped off and the crotch
sucked. No lacerating spasms

sending electrical sparks through the toes.
Stars have those.

What do you have? You're a tool, moon.
Now, noon. There's a hero.

The obvious sun, no bullshit, the enemy
of poets and lovers, sleepers and creatures.

But my lovers have never been able to read
my mind. I've had to learn to be direct.

It's hard to learn that, hard to do.
The sun is worth ten of you.

You don't hold a candle
to that complexity, that solid craze.

Like an animal carcass on the road at night,
picked at by crows,

haunting walkers and drivers. Your face
regularly sliced up by the moving

frames of car windows. Your light is drawn,
quartered, your dreams are stolen.

You change shape and turn away,
letting night solve all night's problems alone.

WHY IS THE COLOR OF SNOW?
Brenda Shaughnessy

Let's ask a poet with no way of knowing.
Someone who can give us an answer,
another duplicity to help double the world.

What kind of poetry is all question, anyway?
Each question leads to an iceburn,
a snownova, a single bed spinning in space.

Poet, Decide! I am lonely with questions.
What is snow? What isn't?
Do you see how it is for me.

Melt yourself to make yourself more clear
for the next observer.
I could barely see you anyway.

A blizzard I understand better,
the secrets of many revealed as one,
becoming another on my only head.

It's true that snow takes on gold from sunset
and red from rearlights. But that's occasional.
What is constant is white,

or is that only sight, a reflection of eyewhites
and light? Because snow reflects only itself,
self upon self upon self,

is a blanket used for smothering, for sleeping.
For not seeing the naked, flawed body.
Concealing it from the lover curious, ever curious!

Who won't stop looking.
White for privacy.
Millions of privacies to bless us with snow.

Don't we melt it?
Aren't we human dark with sugar hot to melt it?
Anyway, the question—

if a dream is a construction then what
is not a construction? If a bank of snow
is an obstruction, then what is not a bank of snow?

A winter vault of valuable crystals
convertible for use only by a zen
sun laughing at us.

Oh Materialists! Thinking matter matters.
If we dream of snow, of banks and blankets
to keep our treasure safe forever,

what world is made, that made us that we keep
making and making to replace the dreaming at last.
To stop the terrible dreaming.

SIX APOLOGIES, LORD
Olena Kalytiak Davis

I Have Loved My Horrible Self, Lord.
I Rose, Lord, and I Rose, Lord, And I,
Dropt. Your Requirements, Lord. 'Spite Your Requirements, Lord,
I Have Loved The Low Voltage Of The Moon, Lord,
Until There Was No Moon Intensity Left, Lord, No Moon Intensity Left
For You, Lord. I Have Loved The Frivolous, The Fleeting,
      The Frightful
Clouds. Lord, I Have Loved Clouds! Do Not Forgive Me, Do Not
Forgive Me LordandLover, HarborandMaster, GuardianandBread,
      Do Not.
Hold Me, Lord, O, Hold Me

Accountable, Lord. I Am
Accountable. Lord.

Lord It Over Me,
Lord It Over Me, Lord. Feed Me

Hope, Lord. Feed Me
Hope, Lord, Or Break My Teeth.

Break My Teeth, Sir,

In This My Mouth.

LOOK AT LESBIA NOW!
Olena Kalytiak Davis

and look at lesbia now! she's said farewell
to her face: dark circled
nipples down and dark
she's even let the hair grow back down there.
right, she's not a real blonde, and
no one's knocking at her door anymore.
we all knew it would turn out like this.

o lesbia, daughter of____and wife of_____and mistress of_____
mother of_____, ha! ceded what? the one so valued
what she had on her once pretty mind
she traded in everyone for that? did you hear
she wouldn't have a baby with her lover
even if he promised to keep it in a tent out back?
so he left.
have you seen her walking alone thru this black and white town
her pink i-pod playing ryan adams, spoon, rilo kiley,
lucinda, arcade fire, the silver jews, mark mulcahy,
yeah, dylan; sufjan stevens, even,
wearing her usual yellow-pink-blue woolen cap?

let the kindergarten parents talk:
yeah, you know, the divorced one, the "poet,"
the one who wears "the jeans,"
circles under her pink eyes, her young boyfriend
just moved back to new york.

WORLD'S BLISS
Alice Notley

The men & women sang & played
they sleep by singing, what
shall I say of the most
poignant on earth the most glamorous
loneliest sought after people
those poets wholly beautiful
desolate aureate, death is a
powerful instinctive emotion—
but who would be released from
a silver skeleton? gems
& drinking cups—This
skull is Helen—who would not
be released from the
Book of Knowledge? Why
should a maiden lie on a moor
for seven nights & a day? And
he is a maiden, he is & she
on the grass the flower the spray
where they lie eating primroses
grown crazy with sorrow & all
the beauties of old—oh each poet's a
beautiful human girl who must die.

OUR VIOLENT TIMES
Alice Notley

We had our violent times
  Now in these ones
we have more. No one's against
  it,
Violence is almost not this
No one's movies, books, the
   story

of how we get by. Not against
her personal country's revolution.
Now we have more   Everyone's
   Cold
around within an exterior mind

Too hot, too cold It would be good,
   too,
if you could be prior, in some ways
The ways we were used to you
before just before now blew you
   away. I,

the one I know, will leave again
Forgetting forms, the pieces fall
  of a membrane of rags.

STANZAS BEFORE TIME
John Ashbery

Quietly as if it could be
otherwise, the ocean turns
and slinks back into her panties.

Reefs must know something of this,
and all the incurious red fish
that float ditsily in schools,

wondering which school is best.
I'd take you for a drive
in my flivver, Miss Ocean, honest, if I could.

OF THE "EAST" RIVER'S CHARM
John Ashbery

homage to Samuel Greenberg (1893–1917)

*We read memorial happiness and cover
Our tables with the great blossoms.*
—S.G., "Ballad on Joy"

The teachings, good, bad, or indifferent, were a warning. It wasn't
going to be easy.

Other things too nasty to mention
mottle the chiffon of a chanson
so it can outlast your laundry condition.
In heavy armor's care
the suitors advanced temporarily.
Was it a comment on today's
mistrustingness, some "moreover"?

These are clad in various fleeting robes
that the tenor knows, as he sees them.
Songs are sung by this counterfeit
contralto to words written down,
and in tomorrow's haste forgotten.

So much for our sham naturalism,
ego, my brother, faster of us two.

Of what? Let me then ask you,
as tide picks up tab, river that between us grew,
mere commentary on agile literary thoughts'
dustbin commonplaces. Yet here and there a jewel

gleamed, night's dark fantasy, over before it began.
Hail to something! Let bliss be unbuttoned
in corners of the rash act's explanation of it.

And dyed two, one new, none knew
an honest periphery as other than rind
of rhyme. The perfect attention snowed
in sleep and no one asked their opinion
of the remaining gents, off on a new tangent.
"I have an engagement."

Manna fell to the ground in streamers
and this was OK,
I heard someone say.

Hectored by possibility, beset,
one withdraws into a corner of the inner corral.
Is this what you wished upon me?
Weren't all my cares naked ones,
and I detached, stalking the streets
like some beast?

Weren't we "apprised," hence good for rest
as long as the mirror accepted our tentative
good nature, our composure?
Others than our children chew rubber bands, cursing
not meaning. In the meantime a nap
prepares a surprise,
travels to no end, but we thought we had one,
but it wasn't over—then—yet the possible bares its teeth
in a grin like a long line.

Just a little critical wondering,
and even architecture finally
gives its reluctant consent
to city's barren din.
The inky eye constrains us to a neighbor's
plot, and all swims iridescently,
as though there were no whither,
or backing out of agreement on a good day
in one's unusual situation.

3

LYNN EMANUEL

↓

TOMAŽ ŠALAMUN

↓

THOMAS KANE

↓

BRANDON SOM

↓

FRANCINE J. HARRIS

LIKE GOD,
Lynn Emanuel

you hover above the page staring down
on a small town. Outside a window
some scenery loafs in a sleepy hammock
of pastoral prose and here is a mongrel
loping and here is a train approaching
the station in three long sentences and
here are the people in galoshes waiting.
But you know this story about the galoshes
is really About Your Life, so, like a diver
climbing over the side of a boat and down
into the ocean, you climb, sentence
by sentence, into this story on this page.

You have been expecting yourself
as a woman who purrs by in a dress
by Patou, and a porter manacled to
the luggage, and a man stalking across
the page like a black cloud in a bad mood.
These are your fellow travelers and
you are a face behind or inside these
faces, a heartbeat in the volley of these
heartbeats, as you choose, out of all
the journeys, the journey of a man
with a mustache scented faintly with
Prince Albert. "He must be a secret
sensualist," you think and your awareness
drifts to his trench coat, worn, softened,

and flabby, a coat with a lobotomy, just
as the train pulls into the station.

No, you would prefer another stop
in a later chapter where the climate is
affable and sleek. But the passengers
are disembarking, and you did not
choose to be in the story of the woman
in the white dress which is as cool and
evil as a glass of radioactive milk. You
did not choose to be in the story of the
matron whose bosom is like the prow
of a ship and who is launched toward
lunch at the Hotel Pierre, or even the
story of the dog-on-a-leash, even though
this is now your story: the story of the
person-who-had-to-take-the-train-and-walk-
the-dark-road described hurriedly by
someone sitting at the tavern so you could
discover it, although you knew all along
the road would be there, you, who have
been hovering above this page, holding
the book in your hands, like God, reading.

MY SUBJECTIVITY:
Lynn Emanuel

I tried to flatter myself into extinction;
buried myself alive in a landslide
of disparagement; ran myself into the ground
with my by-now-notorious irony;
slid insincerity's poisonous oils,
bead by shining bead, down along
the hairy taproot; tried to kill, bury,
burn, embalm and erase the outlines,
mummify myself in the damp wrappings
of surrealism, sever and rearrange me
like Stein's cubisms, break, buy
bribe, drive a stake through me;
tried to bleed to death on the machete
of my wit, tried to censor and edit,
rewrite and emend me, tried to swap
my DNA at the DNA supermarket
I read about in Philip K. Dick.
I turned every road into a mobius strip
leading my sorry self back to myself.
So—how did I get loose again—
hauling myself forth over this choppy terrain,
a tug on the rough boulevards of the black river,
steering by its north star
the small, raw planet of my self-loathing
hammered into the night ahead?

HEATED PASSIONS
Tomaž Šalamun

Let's look:
At what split apart.
At what opened bread.
Two loaves of bread, white hands.
Burnt fields, little hands.
At what touches the dream.
Words stick.
You'll forget what you dance off.
What you dance you give away.
Inside here is a castle.
The dampness is practical.
Access is in the apertures.
They break loose from iron and lead, hoops.
A farewell terminates the slide.
Soldiers whoosh out of a village.
The nucleus has been filled, is protected, has a white skin.
Power chews at everything.
What we've carved out will fall.

—Translated from the Slovenian by Joshua Beckman and the author

FLOR ARS HIPPOCRATICA
Tomaž Šalamun

Have you ever seen a domino
going down
how everything falls down
six points zero points
plus an old biscuit
some cheese without holes
some sad tea without lemon

when electricity suddenly gives out
and they wrap you up
and you cannot play fleas anymore
and it snows
and aunt Agatha howls
before the door

the best seems to be the burnistra bush
leaves in the fall
grinding their teeth in a vase
to the last moment
and for a long time we don't know
what will happen
will the vase break

great wisdom is to water the flowers
but they dry up
the chest from Gabrče is drenched
stamps get wet

Derč
photo albums

on the other side grandpa sits
on the sofa made before World War One
cleans his gun
clergy falls
partridges

and other kinfolk
milk cows with awesome speed
learn how to sit properly
because we'll have somehow
to obtain all this past
get rid of these stains
     but aucun sens public of this fairy tale
     no gain in inviting people to lunch

then comes my father
on the lower edge of the painting where there is
St. Vid, hills planted with vine
naked before the door of his house
action of contrition
and weeping nights
because he would like to be proletarian
but then in his midyears
improves rapidly
and decorates the dining room
with his entrance
wrapped up in waterproof canvas
cotton wool in his eyes and says

lemons lemons
or reads something aloud
a woman without a man
is like a vine without a pole
Ero from the other world
Ero from the other world
blue period
or hangs
crazy stiff from the edge
of the vase
but literature is something else
it's altogether another matter to run the state
or grandpa comes
and takes off his hat in such a way
oooo I say oooo
I'm absent minded oblivious
I don't know what I do
and I run real fast
take off my clothes on the way
and jump into bed
and the kinfolk stand around
and proudly sing
oooo what stock

and I turn over
hide behind a barricade
and pull out my COLT
    aucun sens public
    in this art engaged
    there's no damned sport left anywhere

no tramway to Bronowice
no Brandenburg or America

and I go to Krakow, Brugges, or Assisi
Rotterdam
all these damn stale
railway restaurants
Molly stolen from Ferlinghetti
or Christine
all this Barbara
look at these photos
this is your windbreaker
and I feel super great
and I put on my cap

and on my pilgrims I never wear
little spoons newspapers towels
stickers Par avion
kiss says my son
and I bend
and he hangs a strange thing around my neck
on which is written in a child's hand

FALSE DICK

        FLOR

             ARS HIPPOCRATICA

—Translated from the Slovenian by Joshua Beckman and the author

FROM SOMEWHERE STEAM IS DRAWN
Thomas Kane

The man and woman have taken
(I know this!)
to filling their eyes with a hole
in the horse's tongue.
Is it a sugar blight? Or as the scorpion
kept under a drinking glass knows:
avalanche, hawk, Gerd,
and they are penned. Simply, they think, occurring.
From somewhere steam is drawn left
to right, steam is balanced
on a knee, steam waits
at least to be bathed in, under. And later,
they do, and they sleep.
And we will acquit the streetlight
for once being too much on their feet,
because they are, this second,
the muzzle flash made quiet,
the muzzle flash undone
of its first purpose and keeping only
its skin.

SUPPOSE WHAT IS LEFT BEHIND
Thomas Kane

It's that when I see you
I bleed a little,
into the teacup and into the wren's nest.
And even what is mistaken for seed,
we warm,
making always sure
that, here, something grows.

So the Mormon women become learned
of exquisite names. The groundskeeper finds
a new red shirt in the brush pile.

And I bleed a little something extra
into the trumpet, so to bring about
a fury and then a dirge and then
a song you can whistle.

And we will wear gloves

(oh, how we'll wear gloves!)

to make thumb-big playthings
from the fire's leftovers.

UMBRA PENUMBRA
Brandon Som

There's a peasant drowning a litter of kittens
in a well and noting how the trees around him
seem to slip off dark robes and leave them across
the lawn like the clothes of hurried lovers,

and the mouth of the well seems to spell out
astonishment but has little to say about it
unless there is a language of shadow which
we translate by what is swallowed,

listen to like a given moon conversing
with an articulate cloud whose movement
is a mouthful, whose mouth says aloud
a silence and makes a voice out of a silhouette

like a hummingbird stuck in sheets in sunlight
hung on a line, or maybe the forensic of a tree
wrung of its dark, laid out in laymen's terms
without the branches and their arms full of birds

and leaves—the general bramble of detail we concern
ourselves with, as a peasant might, drawing from the well
and into the light a tarpaulin bag with a litter of kittens,
looking for movement, listening for murmur.

IDENTITY POEM
Brandon Som

Jesus was fond of knock knock jokes and not so much wine, except maybe wine made from certain flowers, lilac or dandelion. It is Christian to say what you mean, which would suggest what you mean is always waiting to be announced, the way the archangel Gabriel came to Mary, nervous, as I understand it, with the task of announcing the birth of the baby Jesus. We say *come out with it, come clean* because meaning, like Mary, is pregnant, labored; and immaculate conception is in some sense, coming clean in such a way that it doesn't get around, that it is kept quiet or maybe just kept between angels. As I understand it, Jesus one evening came upon two girls catching crickets by lanterns. They were telling knock knock jokes. It was April, so they had blossoms, lilac or dandelion, stuck to the bottoms of their bare feet. And the angels, who always have something to say, and a quiet despair for the things they have to say, which is why they are angels, were now silent in the limbs of an olive tree, watching Jesus tell his knock knock joke to two girls, who asked, in unison, and without hesitation, *who's there.*

RIDING THE RICHEST
(AFTER DAMOCLES)
OF NORTH AMERICA
francine j. harris

i alone under a hair. seized sword to hang there.
i hate the horse's hair. bunched or pared to string.

it is both weak and strong, and so suspends the
blade tied there. one hair. one horse's hair. i alone

sit with my head howling there. a hair. a horse hair.
a single strand tying up an unsheathed glitter

a sword that must soon easily swing. in the dusk
it weighs a mare, collects the air, sticks the sands

and swells there. for all who say time
is dreamed, weigh it now. another specked

debris stuck breeze in a castle's tongue, encrusted
frieze, shafts the engraver moved these moments

to carve out and ink deep. had he not grooved
and etched this metal, i might live. had i never

reached for what was never there, i might not notice
how strong a single strand, how the draft drams

per second, slits it to its ragged tear.

IN
francine j. harris

The body starts a wind when it gets broken into. At night, when the
    leaves can't sleep,
the black bark is one eye open and the snap vine dozes with its thorn
    in reach.

You come. Ready to kill for a seed. A nickel. A splash of sap from a
    dead tree.
You wear orange. You walk up, skip. You're the big, sad juice. In
    summer, you knock.
God forbid it roots. Puts itself alone between door and the sweat,
    sweet night.

We don't always think in locks. Or iron, we set up house to bring.
    Dim it warm to want.
When the windows won't open, we restless with our noses pressing
    past the screen.

That's the color of nothing so hot. You bring some buddy to make it
    like poker,
roulette. You bet. Hurl body into stove, you win on how long dead
    weight would take.
You bash blood with glass from instant coffee. So mornings, she jerks
    to light.

4

DENIS JOHNSON

↓

MICHAEL BURKARD

↓

PATRICK LAWLER

↓

LINDA TOMOL PENNISI

↓

MARY STEBBINS

UPON WAKING
Denis Johnson

at the far edge of earth, night
is going away. another
poem begins. slumped over

the typewriter i must get this
exactly, i want to make it
clear this morning that your

face, as it opens
from its shadow, is more
perfect than yesterday; and

that the light, as it
hesitates over the approach
of your smile, has given this

aching bed more than warmth,
more than poems; someway

a generous rose, or a very
delicate arrangement of sounds,
has come to peace in this new room.

UNTITLED
Denis Johnson

Stranger and stranger to one another
waitress on her hands and knees to brush
the carpet underneath a booth. You know—
crawling around on all fours like a dog

underneath a booth etcetera
to be human—to crawl—to

walk through broken glass with gory feet.

People crying on airplanes,
weeping seven miles above the ground,
the grief
taller than Mt. Everest:

People on the street thinking:
I wanted this. And now it's a cloud of chalk.

A pile of blood and guts and torn bones thinking
how beautiful is the tiger who killed me

the shit/ of days

IN THIS STRANGE TIME
(AN UNWRITTEN GOGOL STORY)
Michael Burkard

greta said if you are not writing for the
revolution it is unnecessary writing - and
her brother was a harmless lunatic - but
to tell the truth you never know - the pie
did taste good - his wife had made it - he
hadn't made much of anything except me -
but he failed to understand at the strange time
in maine when they lived nearby where they
still live that i hadn't made much either - or
depending on how you could calculate the gain
he might have come out ahead then - fact of a
marriage which seemed intact - on his way to
a degree in forestry which is what he wanted -
as a matter of fact in this strange time they
already owned their cabin/house - he loved
the woods - she loved him back - some of
us lived in or near the hospitals we worked
at - some quit jobs in theoretical math to
stand side-by-side with the proletariat in
the shoe factories - to work from there - from
the inside - some of us took our love into isolated
territories with books of poems by the likes of
john berryman and robert duncan - two among
many poets we did not and never did understand -
but felt we had to - and did our best to pass this
forced feeling on - imagine the tightness in these
conversations! - like an unwritten gogol story in

which visiting hunters break all the rules and don't
abide by the guide at all - and the guide has a silly
russian surname - mucky muckiovich - and this is
the laugh they have on "mucky" when they gather
the fowl and geese and birds the hunters have shot
to death on a relentless and then drunken sunday
afternoon near vladivastock - "mucky" becomes the
joke so that even the new blood on the trees and
grassy fields does not have to be paid attention -
and they the hunters can return to the city without
hearing the knock of the boat knocking at night
in duncan's wonderful set of structure(s) of rime - at the hotel
wilmington (his locale for one) - just like the knocking
and the boat knocking are his locales too - that was
all that was felt - if gogol had tried the story out....
but we can't fault him - life becomes subtraction and
pain and forgiveness much sooner than we think -
at least one of the hunters thought he dreamt that
a few nights later when stars were out and the new
moon was rising and a boat coughed - at least he
thought he dreamt it before he forgot - and before
he feasted on a father nightingale he had shot

NO ONE
Michael Burkard

Well, yes, you were immobile in the mathematical
classroom. You could be on the sea, very well in fact,
but you were afraid to be in it. Yet you also knew
you knew something of the sea, something believable
and invisible, something you just forgot and a gigantic
moment before you forgot it.

One face leads to another just as a pair of shoes
on this side of the one night past full moon suggests
a pair of shoes or socks on the other side of this
moon. And on the other side of the enchanted journey
you must still make, the one through the face and through
the forest of the heart, the one replete with longing

and comedy about longing, the one complete with a foolish
voice over the telephone and a child's wild drawing of
moons and suns half together and half not but wild in the
still enchanted woods, dove and ghosts and doors and one
still face, and this slight suggestion of a question leading
again to the sea, as if you never left the moment forgotten
by the sea, that kiss there, that robbery there, that abuse

there as only the sea could witness for you to keep you still
intact, on the other side if all the time's lips two more friends
tell you yes, and two more friends tell you no. The child
reaches to draw with her left hand, it's an impulse which was
removed for all intents and purposes years ago. Also, her
long silence around food and stones and trees indicates how

something still slightly unknown, like a question, has entered
unseen from the adult world. And it is this feeling of the in-
visible you address after all, because of her, and because of
an equal exhaustion with all complications which drain you but
like the still world lead you even against your own
self-will to the sea. Like a ghost of your own left hand,
and hers also, the child's, waiting for someone who will

appear but who will also not appear, or may not, and take
your hand and kiss it. And take it to the moon, to the fantastic
moon over a fantastic sea, to make your life the invisible box
the dove sleeps upon, the believable sock which weighs night
like a writer misshapen by love and by sticks, by one journey
after another into intuitive space, the time and place of
appearances, the thinking we will count the world and the worlds

if only given time. But who can give us this time? Other than
ourselves, and a feeling we belong to ourselves, and to no one.
And no one would give us this time except the sun and the sea,
the integrated moon, no on understands no one like they do.

THAT WAS ANOTHER PATRICK LAWLER
Patrick Lawler

Remember the Patrick Lawler
who thought he was God's gift
to women? Remember how the women
always hoped he left behind the receipt?

Remember the Patrick Lawler
who couldn't tell the difference
between the body and the spirit?

"There are just too many intangible
walls," he'd say. And his hands
would almost slip through them.

Remember the Patrick Lawler
who was allergic to words?
He had a rash all over his mouth,
sores on his fingers.

Remember the Patrick Lawler
who would send out thank you notes after sex?

Remember the Patrick Lawler
who felt he was saying so many
worthwhile things
he hired a stenographer?

"Notice how gravity,"
the stenographer would write,

"keeps these words from floating
too far from the page."

Remember the Patrick Lawler who
would receive sympathy cards after sex?

Remember the Patrick Lawler,
the street performer—
the claustrophobic mime.

Every time he created
one of those mime boxes
with his hands sliding
over the invisible walls,
he'd have a panic attack.

Most of the Patrick Lawlers are decoys.
The stenographer can never
get used to the silence.

PATRICK LAWLER WRITES
ABOUT "PATRICK LAWLER"
Patrick Lawler

First, Patrick Lawler would never write
a poem called "Patrick Lawler."
That's the first thing. The first clue.
And there are others.
I mean he wouldn't be that pretentious.
That self-obsessed. Self-absorbed. Narcissistic.

The person who says he is Patrick Lawler
does things that Patrick Lawler would never do.

I warn you.
The Patrick Lawler you know is an impostor.
The body that surrounds him
is his, but the insides are not.

The real Patrick Lawler, the one who does not
reside in quotation marks, is being held hostage.
Somewhere. I can assure you there will be
elegantly written ransom notes
with onomatopoeia and subtle internal rhyme.

Remember the Patrick Lawler
who was a ventriloquist.
Remember the Patrick Lawler who stuttered.

Oh, sure, in retrospect, it's easy to see
how we made the mistake. The fake Patrick Lawlers

looked so much like the real thing. Even better.
They carried a stain of authenticity.

Remember when they had the Win-a-Night-with-
Patrick-Lawler Contest. That was a fake Patrick Lawler.

At one time or another, we've all been fooled.

I must admit I myself have been accused of being
a Patrick Lawler impersonator.

I wish he had done something
remarkable or even remarkably mediocre
so there would be more demand for him.
It's hard to justify the attention.

At the Patrick Lawler Impersonator Convention,
they usually complain about the absence of work.
They hate to admit it but sometimes they
think that there are just too many of them.
When they look at all the name tags, it makes them queasy.

Then there is the rumor that Patrick Lawler
has given up being Patrick Lawler.

Here's the evidence: If Patrick Lawler
did not want to be Patrick Lawler,
then why would he write a poem titled "Patrick Lawler"?

Remember the Patrick Lawler Anonymous meetings?
Remember the Patrick Lawler who had lead eyes?

Remember the Patrick Lawler who tried to use
crutches for wings? It was as if someone were holding him
underwater. He forgot he had eyes.

The real Patrick Lawler's life became dependent
on the Patrick Lawler impersonators.
They began to live his life in more meaningful
ways than he himself had ever lived it.

There was no single, solitary, existential, autonomous
Patrick Lawler. Like emergent properties. Like birds.
Like weather. Like a collection of hats. Consciousness
of the whole was more important than the single self.

You always know if it is him because he stands in front of you—
sometimes silvery, sometimes in slow motion—
and he tries to convince you as if it is the most
significant fact he can possibly share with you.

"This 'person' in front of you," he says, "is *not* Patrick Lawler."

CHEW
Linda Tomol Pennisi

That summer she decided to consume all her calories before noon.
It's not that she woke feeling ravenous, but rather that she knew
intuitively that her hunger had shifted, that the shifting required her
to pull the Tupperware bowl from the fridge before 7:00 and carry the
chunked watermelon to the chair where she'd watch Katie and Matt
discuss the source of the White House leak of a CIA agent to the
press. And the fact that her eating could continue through the morn-
ing was in a strange way nourishing in itself, so she'd ignore the piles
of laundry and the flourishing weeds and would only perform tasks
that allowed her to work and eat simultaneously. And though dusting
and Windexing took longer than usual and sometimes her sourdough
toast ended up smelling of Lemon Pledge or ammonia, she found she
could read and write at just about the same pace as always, the stains
adding abstractions of smudged color—mocha or ruby or midnight
blue. And the way a map might instill in one the desire to travel, or
the way stones might encourage one to step across a too-deep stream,
the stains became part of what she was saying, and when she called her
sister and spoke of how her new eating routine fed her, her sister with
great empathy replied, *Sometimes you just gotta chew.*

DOLL REPAIR SHOP
Linda Tomol Pennisi

The dolls displayed leg holes and cracked open heads. One might be tempted to say they were empty, but we knew better, standing there on Oak Street before the smudged glass. It was almost embarrassing, the way we could see deep inside the eye sockets. (Think *Vagina* but don't say it.) The way a bottom lip had split, the way a fly crawled on the cloth where a porcelain chin had ripped away. (Think: *Tomorrow is the day I'll wash the sins beneath my skin.*) We found ourselves studying the bodies in all kinds of light, all kinds of weather. (Think: *I wound the gauze around my wound.*) Snow would darken the already dark places. When rain quivered and slid, we thought the dolls inside the glass were trembling. When sun spilled in, those with open heads toppled toward us like cups of gold light. (Think: *Drink from me wherever I am cracked.*) Often on cloud-shrouded mornings, our small breathing tried to block the wind from seeping in. (Think: *We practiced placing parts of ourselves inside another's body.*) (Think: *Wherever my reflection goes, I will go also.*)

LEAVING A TRAIL
FOR KEITH
Mary Stebbins

I feel it slipping away. Try to burrow back
Into that other place, where we stood
Behind falling water, but the sun, relentless, tugs. Day claims
And wakes me, and sets in motion its machineries. Pulleys
And cogs, flywheels. The small linked gears
Of a thousand choices and mistakes. Hours later,
On a sidewalk between two meetings, I remember.
That place. With you in it. This place, without you,
Has rows of honey locusts and pear trees
With small hard fruit. Bricks set unevenly
In the earth. No rushing water. Walls of stone
And mortar. No hemlocks. No owls. Pigeons
And English sparrows. Rats.
I crumble my crackers and leave a trail. Not to follow it
Back. I'm not that foolish. Instead, I could live among the rats,
Sleep nestled in their sleek fur, deep in their dark burrows,
Hidden in the sewers under the city. Or I could live
With pigeons, starlings and sparrows. Number their hairs
With the touch of my fingers. O love. So sharp. I imagined love
Had nothing to do with me. But I remember drawing you
Toward my lair with its skulls, bones and pelts
Before the wheel of light turned between us. My hand
On the crank of the cable of dream
Keeps winding us closer.

TOWARD YOU
ANOTHER FOR KEITH
Mary Stebbins

Wind expands, full of the smells

of algae, pickerel and clouds, wet on the western sides

of my face and hand. Zebra mussels crunch underfoot.

Waves grind them to powder, changing the color

and texture of the gold that stretches and fades

into far grey. Gulls, perched atop rain-darkened boulders, launch

into mist and circle as I approach. In wet sand, I kneel

to study blue, a rain-glazed crab claw dropped by a gull.

Later, rain peppers the windshield as I drive

along the shore highway. Drying, my face almost disappears,

I roll down the confining window,

spread fingers, thrust into rain, breathe

pickerel and algae again. I don't yet know

that in an hour, I will meet you. Tangle you

forever with falling water, blue crab, wet breath.

Rain grazes my cheek as I hurtle toward you.

5

MARY KARR

↓

COURTNEY QUEENEY

↓

TERRANCE HAYES

↓

A. VAN JORDAN

↓

RUTH ELLEN KOCHER

DISGRACELAND
Mary Karr

Before my first communion at 40, I clung
    to doubt as Satan spider-like stalked
        the orb of dark surrounding Eden
            for a wormhole into paradise.

God had first formed me in the womb
    small as a bite of burger.
        Once my lungs were done
            He sailed a soul like a lit arrow

to inflame me. Maybe that piercing
    made me howl at birth,
        or the masked creatures
            whose scalpel cut a lightning bolt to free me—

I was hoisted by the heels and swatted, fed
    and hauled through rooms. Time-lapse photos show
        my fingers grew past crayon outlines,
            my feet came to fill spike heels.

Eventually, I lurched out to kiss the wrong mouths,
    get stewed, and sulk around. Christ always stood
        to one side with a glass of water.
        I swatted the sap away.

When my thirst got great enough
    to ask, a stream welled up inside;
        some jade wave buoyed me forward;
        and I found myself upright

in the instant, with a garden
       inside my own ribs aflourish. There, the arbor leafs.
             The vines push out plump grapes.
                   You are loved, someone said. Take that

and eat it.

THE FALL AND RISE OF THE DOMESTICALLY VIOLENT EMPIRE
Mary Karr

She fell like a shot bird from a dawn sky, head down, full weight,
with a splash at the end. Fell like a plane shot down—dials twirling

like the skirts of girls on a green field dizzy. *Fall down*,
the teacher once ordered—*duck and cover*. The atomic blast

would blanch skin to bone, and the fields scorch, monkey bars melt,
the tar roads walked to school on—boiling. It was dusk

when he first put his hand over her eyes, *Shield me, love*,
he begged—*from your pure stare*. His mouth fastened on hers,

she exhaled decades of breath held in and fell
as if fired from a cannon and died there in the white sheets,

died in the green granite shower—the mirrored walls
making spirits of them. Later, in the pillow fight, she stood nude

on the bed, the room snowing feathers, and he surrendered—
his hand on his chest cavity, his stare an arrow fleet.

She fell for the look, the line
hook and sinker, the luscious afternoon.

She never dreamed that his hand with its thread count
under Egyptian cotton could ball into a fist and whap so hard a head

he'd just been cradling in his lap—not even a quarrel
in progress. Some misery would pierce him like an oboe note,

and while she slept, that fist would land its blow.
She'd wake to find his eyes all scribbled in as with pencil lead,

and she could not at that point grow small enough—
even coiled on the floor, becoming unborn.

She'd wanted opulent afternoons, the plain work
of assembling stuff bought from Target: and he was a man

who turned the screws flush. She'd never fallen before,
not in rehab—the trust fall, with companions behind her urging.

She'd preferred vertical, thanks. So when she fell, a bomb
from her inner aircraft bay loosed windswept flames,

made scars where her eyes had been.
And even when she knew that dirt would soon

from his shovel spatter her face, she fell—
forgetting she'd once had a laugh that could fill stadiums,

that her hands could lower to a holiday table
rounded by friends and kids a platter of roasted bird

and root vegetables. He stood in the bare living room
swinging an ash bat—his name stamped in gold on it—

and from his diminutive stature and from the great wheel
he described in air she knew some day her head would fly, divorced

from the rest of her. *Never again*, he said weeping
for the umpteenth time—on his knees. *Get up*, she said,

which was what God (to whom she'd been talking)
said in her core, in a voice made temperate by the endlessness

of His vigil, a voice of jasmine and tide heave, of spangled sky
and slow planets turning. *Get up*, He said, *over it,*

out—and the sea spray in her went solid,
the sap went wood. There was heft to her hand

on the doorknob, her feet on the tarmac,
every eye in her blazed open. The gate officer

holding her I.D. declared *Good*
to go. She strapped in, leaned back—did glide

into stellar blue—a silver pindot, a period.
And that fist he'd hit her with was all

she'd left for him to fuck.
#####

THE ANTI-LEADING LADY DISSOCIATES
Courtney Queeney

Some days I approximate a vacant lot.
Instead of fire I have a face—a solid
slow-flowing, a target's white and heart
and near unhittable. There is no heat
or wavelength of radiance to reach me
in my assemblage of bones, the scaffold
that props me upright and adult. I leave
my name at home when I go out in crowds,
swallowing my blank, untutored tongue.
Some lies light, others shadow. My right hand shuns
the left, vocal cords divorce the lungs,
never endings split from the spine. From no one
nothing can be taken. I swear,
there's someone home, but I don't own her.

ELOPING ALONE
Courtney Queeney

Dear Man:

I'm leaving you my overbloomed ghetto of a garden and my spinster
cat. Her hysteria's been scalpeled out and sutured over. I'm taking my
ring finger with me, my whitest sheets.

I realize in an earlier century I would already be installed in the attic
of a luckier sibling with a pair of knitting needles and an obligation
to the bloodiest slaughters, canning vegetables by candlelight while
the others bed down with hot flannel-wrapped bricks at their feet.
I understand in another country I could be killed for flaunting my
delicate wrists and ankles.

But I'm sick of coming over to wash your dishes so you can press
against me from behind, like every unfulfilled naughty housewife
fantasy I ever had. I am too full of tremors, and you don't have
enough years in you.

I hope you find the girl you deserve, the one with no fruit flies,
who'll swell some kids into the world bearing the average of your two
ordinary faces. She'll quiet at night, and wake according to the clock.

These aren't shivers, they're a shaking off. It's a really neat trick I turn,
it's one of my dozen disappearing acts.

Your,

X.

THE BLUE TERRANCE
Terrance Hayes

I come from a long line hollowed out on a dry night,
the first son in a line of someone else's children,
afraid of water, closets, other people's weapons,
hunger and stupidity; afraid of the elderly and the new dead,
bodies tanned by lightening; afraid of dogs without ethos,
each white fang on the long walk home. I believe all the stories
of who I was: a hardback book, a tent behind the house
of a grandmother who was not my grandmother, the smell of beer,
which is a smell like sweat. They say I climbed to the roof
with a box of light bulbs beneath my arm. Before the bricks,
there were trees, before the trees, there were lovers
barely rooted to the field, but let's not talk about them,
it makes me blue. I come from boys throwing rocks
bigger than their fists at the head of the burned girl,
her white legs webbed as lace on a doily. In someone's garage
there was a flashlight on two dogs pinched in heat.
And later, a few of the puppies born dead and too small
to be missed. I come from howls sent up all night and all day,
summers below the hoop and board nailed to a pine tree.
I come from light bulbs glowing with no light and no expressions,
thrown as far as the will allows like a night chore, like a god
changing his mind; from the light broken on the black road
leading to my mother. Tell me what you remember of her
now that her walk is old, now that the bone in her hip strains
to heal its fracture? I come from the hot season
gathering its things and leaving. I come from the dirt road
leading to the paved one. I will not return to the earth
as if I had never been born. I will not wait to become a bird

dark enough to bury itself in midair. I wake up sometimes
in the middle of the country with fur on my neck.
Where did they bury my dog after she hung herself,
and into the roots of what tree are those bones entangled?
I come blessed like a river of black rock, like a long secret,
and the kind of kindness like a door that is closed
but not locked. Yesterday I was nothing but a road
heading four ways. When I threatened to run away
my mother said she would take me wherever I wanted to go.

GHAZAL-HEAD
Terrance Hayes

You no good fork sucker, that's what.
You no good backscratcher, that's what.

A blue thumbnail. An old light fixture. A toy-like hammer.
A glass or pitcher. Bend your fingers, that's what.

You're one of those sleepers. Those pod people
Poking their noses, those nose blowers, that's what.

I could care less for your deluxe vacuum.
Suck your own luck you no good Hoover, that's what.

Gulp, gulp, I yelled at your mouth when I saw it walking
Across the room like a no good rumor, that's what.

No count number. Indentured mumbler.
Black shoe stumbler. Beer belly bumbler, that's what.

And I know you know I know and I could care less.
Your ailments into amens; angst into anger, that's what.

Slow down, I told the boy with the knife.
Give me a hug, I told that mother hugger, that's what.

I lied, what about it? I loitered too. Like dust.
I did what you did like a no good mirror, that's what.

What about it, po' mouth? You no good goody goody.
What about it? I know what I said. Lover, that's what.

"FROM"
A. Van Jordan

from (prep.) 1. Starting at (a particular place or time): As in, John was *from* Chicago, but he played guitar straight *from* the Delta; he wore a blue suit *from* Robert Hall's; his hair smelled like coconut; his breath, like mint and bourbon; his hands felt like they were *from* slave times when he touched me—hungry, stealthy, trembling. 2. Out of: He pulled a knot of bills *from* his pocket, paid the man and we went upstairs. 3. Not near to or in contact with: He smoked the weed, but, surprisingly, he kept it *from* me. He said it would make me too self-conscious, and he wanted those feelings as far away *from* us as possible; he said a good part of my beauty was that I wasn't conscious of my beauty. Isn't that funny? So we drank Bloody Mothers (Hennessey and tomato juice), which was hard to keep *from* him—he always did like to drink. 4. Out of the control or authority of: I was released *from* my mama's house, *from* dreams of hands holding me down, *from* the threat of hands not pulling me up, *from* the man that knew me, but of whom I did not know; released *from* the dimming of twilight, *from* the brightness of morning; *from* the love I thought had to look like love; *from* the love I thought had to taste like love, *from* the love I thought I had to love like love. 5. Out of the totality of: I came *from* a family full of women; I came *from* a family full of believers; I came *from* a pack of witches—I'm just waiting to conjure my powers; I came *from* a legacy of lovers—I'm just waiting to seduce my seducer; I came *from* a pride of proud women, and we take good care of our young. 6. As being other or another than: He couldn't tell me *from* his mother; he couldn't tell me *from* his sister; he couldn't tell me *from* the last woman he had before me, and why should he—we're all the same woman. 7. With (some person, place, or thing) as the instrument, maker, or source: Here's a note *from* my mother, and you can take it as advice *from* me: A weak lover is more dangerous than a strong enemy; if you're going to love someone, make sure you know where they're coming *from*. 8. Because of: Becoming an alcoholic, learning to walk away, being a good speller, being good in bed, falling in love—they all come *from* practice. 9. Outside or beyond the possibility of: In the room, he kept me *from* leaving by keeping me curious; he kept me *from* drowning by holding my breath in his mouth; yes, he kept me *from* leaving till the next day when he said *Leave*. Then, he couldn't keep me *from* coming back.

THE ATOM DISCOVERS STRING THEORY
DC COMICS, JUNE – JULY 1964, #13
"WEAPON WATCHES OF CHRONOS"
A. *Van Jordan*

My plans were simply to escape
The grip of Chronos, my foe
Who manipulates time and bends
It around me like a cage

With no space between the bars.
Shrinking to the size of no observed
Size, shrinking to a particle with mass
But no weight, lighter than light,

Was not the plan; but there I was:
So small I was lost between dimensions.
Space was merely a grid leading to more
Grids. Our three dimensions were

Doors leading to six more doors, opening
And closing with the force of a gale
Through one and the force
Of silent kisses through another,

Oscillating faster than I could comprehend.
And if these dimensions were hidden
Inside the crenulated folds of ours, I realized
I had disappeared. I thought

I was merely running away to come back

To catch my villain by surprise.
I thought I was tricking the trickster,
Slipping his snare, but I simply ensnared

Myself. I was lost in the dark, jumping
Between lanes stretched before me
Like violin strings. Every move
Was vibrato—at first, andante, then,

Andante un poco allegretto. Yes,
I was scared of the world within my own
In which even my tiny flashlight's beam
Bent toward my boots in fear, it seemed,

As I moved along the spectrum,
Plucking my way through the strands
Of force and matter under my feet,
Which were now, all at once, running closer

To and farther away from the answers
That would tie my world together.

ISSUES INVOLVING INTERPRETATION
Ruth Ellen Kocher

The word has no life of its own
despite what the writer tells you.
Behind the sword is no quivering
hand worn into life's hilt, no arm
swaying the wind in dying movement.
There is only the word, sword.

Outside, the trees live without language
and tip toward whatever sun manages
through a thinning atmosphere of dust,
ice, and vapor. The life of each branch
balances on what the tree affords it. The soil
holds the tree without language or pity.

But there is no tree in this poem, only
the word, tree. There is no speaker who
entreats you to imagine the tree standing
solitary in a green field, specked with clover
rising up in tufts of almost transparent cream.
There is no field. There is no clover, no green.

But you listen, anyway. Hear her voice
follow you into the afternoon, imagine language
crosses a clearing, the stark way a thing reveals
when thinned clouds expose better light. You
are the tree, tip toward words as they overcome
absence, bring outward your inner forms.

41
Ruth Ellen Kocher

open your mouth to a whisper that escapes the soft oval within you,
the small harp in your throat, the thin vibration of your lungs
        strung tight.

your mouth around it understands the vacuous want of space,
understands the glacier's blue repose, the horse's gleaming flank
an underbelly of its diction, the soft pile of its back swelling
        into open

air and expanding. a whisper, a vapor expelled into a gully's mist,
        its body
ballooned and dashed against cliffs that, in return, echo back its low

seduction to a landscape that fails, only, because it does not know
        your name,
your curved calf, does not hold your footprints in its muddy palms.
        we can

remain like this, you and i, hobbled in this quietude, or you can open
your mouth to desert dunes moved by a wind indifferent to
        the smallest

thing that breathes there—a whisper, a violet evening that opens into
        near silence,
swallows the frigid corners with a widening warmth expressed from
        deep within you,
a heat taken up by your heart's task to quake its thunder and
        blood through

your veins, and then, words that realize the dream of pulsed rhythm
      in your
wrists—the way the body wants for syllable, actuates our tranquil
      grammar.

6

YUSEF KOMUNYAKAA

↓

TRACY K. SMITH

↓

TINA CHANG

↓

LARISSA SZPORLUK

↓

HEIDI JOHANNESEN POON

THANKS
Yusef Komunyakaa

Thanks for the tree
between me & a sniper's bullet.
I don't know what made the grass
sway seconds before the Viet Cong
raised his soundless rifle.
Some voice always followed,
telling me which foot
to put down first.
Thanks for deflecting the ricochet
against that anarchy of dusk.
I was back in San Francisco
wrapped up in a woman's wild colors,
causing some dark bird's love call
to be shattered by daylight
when my hands reached up
& pulled a branch away
from my face. Thanks
for the vague white flower
that pointed to the gleaming metal
reflecting how it is to be broken
like mist over the grass,
as we played some deadly
game for blind gods.
What made me spot the monarch
writhing on a single thread
tied to a farmer's gate,
holding the day together
like an unfingered guitar string,

is beyond me. Maybe the hills
grew weary & leaned a little in the heat.
Again, thanks for the dud
hand grenade tossed at my feet
outside Chu Lai. I'm still
falling through its silence.
I don't know why the intrepid
sun touched the bayonet,
but I know that something
stood among those lost trees
& moved only when I moved.

FROM LOVE IN THE TIME OF WAR
Yusef Komunyakaa

The jawbone of an ass. A shank
braided with shark teeth. A garrote.
A shepherd's sling. A jagged stone
that catches light & makes warriors
dance to a bull-roarer's lamentation.
An obsidian ax. A lion-skin drum
& reed flute. A nightlong prayer
to gods stopped at the mouth of a cave.

The warrior-king summons one goddess
after another to his bloodstained pallet.
If these dear ones live inside his head
they still dress his wounds with balms
& sacred leaves, & kiss him
back to strength, back to a boy.

                *   *   *

Here, the old masters of Shock & Awe
huddle in the war room, talking iron,
fire & sand, alloy & nomenclature.
Their hearts lag against the bowstring
as they daydream of Odysseus's bed.
But to shoot an arrow through the bulls'-eye
of twelve axes lined up in a row
is to sleep with one's eyes open. Yes,

of course, there stands lovely Penelope
like a trophy, still holding the brass key

against her breast. How did the evening star
fall into that room? Lost between plot
& loot, the plucked string turns into a lyre
humming praises & curses to the unborn.

      *   *   *

Someone's beating a prisoner.
Someone's counting red leaves
falling outside a clouded window
in a secret country. Someone holds back
a river with a song, but the next rabbit jab
makes him piss on the stone floor.
The interrogator orders the man
to dig his grave with a tea spoon.

The one he loves, her name
died last night on his tongue.
To revive it, to take his mind off
the electric wire, he almost said,
There's a parrot in a blue house
that knows the password, a woman's name.

DUENDE
Tracy K. Smith

1.

The earth is dry and they live wanting.
Each with a small reservoir
Of furious music heavy in the throat.
They drag it out and with nails in their feet
Coax the night into being. Brief believing.
A skirt shimmering with sequins and lies.
And in this night that is not night,
Each word is a wish, each phrase
A shape their bodies ache to fill—

> *I'm going to braid my hair*
> *Braid many colors into my hair*
> *I'll put a long braid in my hair*
> *And write your name there*

They defy gravity to feel tugged back.
The clatter, the mad slap of landing.

2.

And not just them. Not just
The ramshackle family, the *tíos*,
Primitos, not just the *bailaor*
Whose heels have notched
And hammered time
So the hours flow in place
Like a tin river, marking
Only what once was.

Not just the voices scraping
Against the river, nor the hands
nudging them farther, fingers
like blind birds, palms empty,
echoing. Not just the women
with sober faces and flowers
in their hair, the ones who dance
as though they're burying
memory—one last time—
beneath them.

              And I hate to do it here.
To set myself heavily beside them.
Not now that they've proven
The body a myth, parable
For what not even language
Moves quickly enough to name.
If I call it pain, and try to touch it
With my hands, my own life,
It lies still and the music thins,
A pulse felt for through garments.
If I lean into the desire it starts from—
If I lean unbuttoned into the blow
Of loss after loss, love tossed
Into the ecstatic void—
It carries me with it farther,
To chords that stretch and bend
Like light through colored glass.
But it races on, toward shadows
Where the world I know
And the world I fear
Threaten to meet.

3.

There is always a road,
The sea, dark hair, *dolor*.

Always a question
Bigger than itself—

> *They say you're leaving Monday*
> *Why can't you leave on Tuesday?*

ASTRAL
Tracy K. Smith

It begins with a finger on the switch,
Eyes open in the dark until I see—what
Do I see? That empty scrap and scrabble
Etched in static above the bed.
But isn't it something? A baby's thigh,
A carriage? A half-scallop with a lady in it?
The heart slows. A procession through snow.
All that bad tv, weak signals. But I follow.
What collides? What is this real thing
That happens only at night?

* * *

My husband is far off and thinks of me
In the past tense. I wept. I was. You
Lean into the curve your wife makes sleeping.
She is in Buenos Aires, always Buenos Aires
When she sleeps, your heft a bundle she must carry
From café to café. A child or a bag of pastries.
Her jewelry glints in daylight. What if
My foot presses down onto the white blanket
Of moonlight patching your sheet?
Where am I that I am here?

In the mountains of Wyoming
A trout looks up through the roof
Water makes. Feathers, fur, a fine
Thread of invisible chord skirt

The surface, and the trout's mind
Makes the sign for fly. Who knows
How this is done? Whether the trout
Sees the flit, the flicker on water
And recalls the brief satisfaction
Of air, the knot of legs,
Wings that collapse? And so
It leaps with its whole body.
Inveterate. And your biceps
Tighten, don't they? For a moment
You become the fish—pure muscle,
Desire tethered to desire. A stone
Skipped across this same river.
You tug back, sink the hook.

When my husband sleeps,
He makes the shirred murmur
Of sea and shore at night.
He is racing toward a gold
Disc that sits at the distance
Like an enormous yolk. It drops
Quickly, and the water glows hot.
There is barely time, he knows.
When my husband brushes
His knuckles against her thigh,
The woman beside him smiles.
They loll on the sand.
Tiny waves nip at their feet.

Sirens wail and blare in Buenos Aires
Where your wife has caused a man's

Heart to sputter & choke, her fingers
Are that delicate. Is it her you feel
Now, when I touch the lids of your
Sleeping eyes? Your face is empty,
As if there really is a soul
That roams the planet at night. Yours
Must be heavy. Why else would you look
Now like a vacant doll, like you might rise
At the slightest effort, the faintest breeze?
And distant. Farther than the river,
Than the trout now, which has left
The river forever, unless there is a river
It remembers and traces with the memory
Of its own slick shape, terse weight.
Maybe desire is nothing but memory,
And we dream only what has already been.

Your wife falls in love with a dark man
Who leads her from ballroom to ballroom.
Their love is a slow tango. They dance
Without pause, knowing that one day
A bell will wake them, that she'll weep,
And he'll recede into the traffic of Buenos Aires,
Waving with his one raised arm
Like a figurine in an aquarium. My husband
Kicks at the sand and traces the shape
Of the woman beside him. A silhouette
Against the night sky. So many stars.
Her long hair moves like a curtain
In the breeze. *Soon*, she tells him,
All the sand will be rearranged.

NAMING THE LIGHT
Tina Chang

My beautiful brother opens the garage door
on a Saturday morning, taking out the tools
to rake the leaves around the gated house.

He hates this job but does it anyway,
the way he makes his breakfast before daylight.
He gets up as my father would, without question.

The idea of infinity haunts me. The dark days boundless.
My brother raking the leaves on an autumn day
equals the loneliness I feel, waking up

on my mattress, the light not light yet.
My brother that comes in from the cold now
is the same brother that came in from the snow

20 years ago, pounding his boots to wet the carpet,
pieces of frost clinging to his winter hat. Taking off
his gloves, he lets the house warm him. The idea

of the present is that we will last, or that the minutes
might outlive us, that the universe within each
veined leaf will surpass the present tense.

When evening comes, lights dim from each window.
A figure stands by a lamp just about to shut it.
In this moment, it seems as if this job is important,

that if the light fades it will be one less marker of the night.
I realign the pens on my desk as if realigning the stars.
My brother once put his name on a slip of paper.

In his boyhood hand, he wrote his name, *Vincent*,
in script, the slanted letters uncertain and fragile.
Today, I found his name in my pocket.

REIGN
Tina Chang

The empress dowager was fourth in line,
peeled from her clothing, placed
at the foot of the emperor's bed.

Should she have a weapon, she would have
no clothes to conceal it. All she would have
were her long fingernails as sex toy or talon.

Bearing a son, she was promoted,
the eunuchs conspired with her.
She ruled the country, and didn't want

anything back but jewels, cutting away
into everything. When the emperor died, her son
was next in line; she fed him with whores, opium

until he died too. She was left in power
with her vaults of gems gleaming.
She loved the poached eggs in the golden bowl,

nothing else mattered but the hundred dishes
on lacquer plates. She was beautiful once
and beauty made her master.

She was the one with all the hands, the ghosts in red,
the walk through the walled city, the willful
assassination of love, the famine

which fed her, made her want nothing more
from her own kind. She looked at the mirror,
a hollowed face watching the monsoons

sweep away the houses in the heat.
The weeds rose up through her body,
breaking her body, tearing through.

She loved once, a theater of fantastic concerns.
The sky was a careful picture
and she paid one hundred artists to get it right.

They each had a talent for color, shape, texture;
locked in a windowless room, they imagined clouds
searing through solid mountain. The artists listened

to her dying voice and tried to achieve it.
She had all killed but one.
She paid the best architect in the country

to make her room something from a page in heaven
so that when she opened her door, she could swear
she was dying in riches dripping from her living hand.

A century later when they dynamited her grave,
her teeth were still in tact, with an expression that was pure,
paramount, her nostrils and mouth stuffed with diamonds.

LEAVING THE ECCENTRIC
Larissa Szporluk

The queenfish visits the spring
every spring, and she does it alone,
carried away from her silvery coast,
the blue drum region, carried away
by the aerial ocean above,
the dipping and rising, sidling along
saddles of thawing mountains,
thrashing through caribou tracks,
past dens of bears, exposing herself
to countless dangers, because of a whim
to be in the iciest possible
water, up to her eyes in the highest
spring, spring on the fringe of fish
civilization, spring where the king,
who loves her, lives, year after year,
for this single visit, the look of pain
on his outer face as he remembers
he should eat her. That's when the queen
takes her leave, flapping her battered
tail, slipping her body under. That's when
the one who loves her screams,
sharding the spring with manic octaves
(like bells of mules setting hills
ringing with each beating)—what else
can they do but follow its law
in wonder, the law of the sun
which burns, pulling the world to it,
the paradox of equinox, when light

and dark, and less and great, are all
the same, and every answer
strings its question up in space:
Are blood and love just things that run,
and if they're not, do they belong
to what they are, or to the place
they're running to or from, and what
if that's the point of life, to turn
your back into your front
and mount the beast again?

THE RECLUSE
Larissa Szporluk

Light rose like a bee in the early
watery twirl of the bird. In her bath,
my rosewater daughter screamed
and twirled without feeling grief.
Like the moon, she could mate
with the first early bird or the bee's
first mate, and twirl like wool,
razed too deep, my daughter,
that sheep, my grief, her watery
mate in the heat, her early-bird
scream in the moon's rose-twirl,
her youth as she bathes in the light
of my hate, like a bee without feeling
its feet, or me, my grief at losing
my youth in the loom of the scream
that spooled me out like a fledgling
kite from my heavenly term in hell's
cocoon, and followed me down
with watery teeth, and gnawed my
hide until I was too weak, to stop her,
my daughter, from parting my walls,
grazing my brain like a thorn.

UNIVERSITY HOSPITAL PATHOLOGY LAB
Heidi Johannesen Poon

A marionette of the rib cage
is hanging
in the cadaver room.

No one believes it can sing
or can't sing.
It isn't made to,

only to teach the pieces
posited in the chest.
In order to leave

for the day
allegements must be made:
interns must guess

what can and cannot fly
in a living thing.
Must guess which souls can get by

when they are held inside,
the tissues fed;
what in retrospect

is suicide: blue and white
prayers puffed out again
before they petrify;

so they look down
one more time,
before they leave for the day,

memorize, because it means so much
to be taken outside.
Like birds, like wildlife.

FEAST
Heidi Johannesen Poon

The town is already set
for Christmas. The timer sends
Bach to the church bell

and people still come in, tempted
to find the old pews.
The pigeons, without coming in,

are a custom too
and heavily marked in a forum
they're losing,

desire for sugar making them,
right on the street,
backs and beaks and wings.

7

MICHAEL ONDAATJE

↓

LISA ROBERTSON

↓

CAROLINE BERGVALL

↓

RODRIGO TOSCANO

↓

KAIA SAND

DRIVING WITH DOMINIC
IN THE SOUTHERN PROVINCE
WE SEE HINTS OF THE CIRCUS
Michael Ondaatje

The tattered Hungarian tent

A man washing a trumpet
at a roadside tap

Children in the trees,

one falling
into the grip of another

STEP
Michael Ondaatje

The ceremonial funeral structure for a monk
made up of thambili palms, white cloth
is only a vessel, disintegrates

completely as his life.

The ending disappears,
replacing itself

with something abstract
as air, a view.

All we'll remember in the last hours
is an afternoon—a lazy lunch
then sleeping together.

Then the disarray of grief.

       *   *   *

On the morning of a full moon
in a forest monastery
thirty women in white
meditate on the precepts of the day
until darkness.

They walk those abstract paths
their complete heart

their burning thought focused
on this step, then *this* step.

In the red brick dusk
of the Sacred Quadrangle,
among holy seven-storey ambitions
where the four Buddhas
of Polonnaruwa
face out to each horizon,
is a lotus pavilion.

Taller than a man
nine lotus stalks of stone
stand solitary in the grass,
pillars that once supported
the floor of another level.

(The sensuous stalk
the sacred flower)

How physical yearning
became permanent.
How desire became devotional
so it held up your house,
your lover's house, the house of your god.

And though it is no longer there,
the pillars once let you step
to a higher room
where there was worship, lighter air.

[UNTITLED]
Lisa Robertson

And if I become unintelligible to myself
Because of having refused to believe
I transcribe a substitution
Like the accidental folds of a scarf.
From these folds I make persons
Perfect marriage of accident and need.
And if I become unintelligible to myself
Because of having refused a style
I transcribe a substitution
To lose the unattainable.
Like the negligent fall of a scarf
Now I occupy the design.

MY FRIEZE
FROM DEBBIE: AN EPIC
Lisa Robertson

My very marrow! When I pose in that

intolerably cloistered skirt like

fidelity is sutured to armour

's louche preposition not opacity

not horror not human nor the frayed trope

of rome coiled into my body—ah

only the perspex is really equal

only the perspex is really equal

in either deferral or fantasy

I sit down on the pink satin lips in

extricably to commission my frieze:

someone drags an amazon like a dead

a kneeling amazon a fallen a

mazon who defended by a comrade

herself against an amazon at a

fallen amazon an amazon facing

backwards an amazon armed with a word

pulling an amazon treading down an

amazon an amazon with a mounted

amazon from behind by an ama

zon over a fallen amazon an

amazon overcoming striking down

an amazon an amazon striking

from behind another amazon to

reciprocate in some hour's pealing

soul soul the small movement of streamers painted

spasms of fleshing stuffing themselves into

air fucking gorgeousness garments of

perspex rubbings in this version call it

bureaucracy Virgil let's just sit past

luxe in that calm way open our decade

slips when I confiscate love's shutter to

rhythm when through the casual banner

my object dominion with medium

of torso of wire after lilac with leather

ette and resistance phones seven worlds of

difficulty and shame and newness this

corrosions of pixils at lilac

is not my videosoul this—where I

confect the speaking kiss reconscious, brim

the lucid technology of affect

and with vainglorious commitment—is

for you.

GONG
11 JULY 2003 – 48 LINES
Caroline Bergvall

My mother is playful, has a generous spirit, who teaches integrity.

My father is steadfast, remains alert, who seeks inner calm.

The woman with the white hair shows me how to whistle
    two fingers pushed against the tongue.

The boy on the island has a salty mouth.

Alicia wants to pull me up into her bed.

My grandmother reads Teilhard de Chardin, boils broccoli on Sundays.

Dominique explores without restriction, flesh takes hold in my body
    turns as it turns to love.

The boy in the back of the car with his hand on my breast.

Guri is my first collaborator who's precise and works without gloss.

My grandmother smells of rose perfume, lives 33 rue de Vaugirard.

Derek Jarman tends an open garden on his illness.

Monique Wittig writes fiercely
    this great need in the love of women
        this great violence towards the love in women.

My teacher doesn't intercept the course of sex, lets the children play.

Cathy de Monchaux' sculptures are doorjoins
    rows of chalked up leather-pouches
        crushed lips, whitened scarabs.

My doctor applies ointments, heals physical and emotional shame.

The boy on the carpet with the smooth chest and his cock in the
    evening air.

The voluptuous girl in the room at the far end of the corridor
    has had us all.

Cherry wears a tartan at the opening.

Rod is soft and amused.

Rachel Whiteread casts resins in negative space, shimmer in the
    gallery.

My sister has fire in the heart, understands fear and takes her chances.

Jo is constant in friendship, shares in salacious tales and trains her body.

Stacy writes the grammar of birds, the suddenness of diving.

The dry sound of snow.

Morton Feldman in the Rothko Chapel.

Sally's hair is red and full.

The boy in the square is gentle and playful,
    the grass is moist under the moon.

Krzysztof Wodiczko provokes dialogue through
    high-tech Mouthpieces, Alien Staffs.

Romana is thoughtful, works from doubt as much as conviction.

My brother is opinionated and good-humoured, keeps his door open.

Cris is joyous about art, eats with friends, collects all kinds of pieces.

The girl laughing ejaculates in my hand.

Felix Gonzales-Torres leaves the fewest of traces.

The beautiful girl spreads over me in the American hotel, I'm drinking
    too much, I'm generating a lot of fear.

Amin Maalouf reads the Rubaiyyat from Paris.

Lorca enters the song.

Cixous climbs the ladder of her name.

The black virgin is in everything.

My healer encourages meditation, demands responsibility.

My aunt keeps the Bhagavad-Gita in her car-door.

Harriet speaks her mind, holds her head up.

The first global march, 15 Feb. 2003.

My admiration for Arundhati Roy's positioning as a public intellectual.

Edmond Jabès writes that a writer is accountable
     also for what they choose not to write, for silence kept.

Hiroshi Sugimoto photographs seascapes, cinema screens, architecture
     radiant light in time
          "just air and water".

Josie holds emotional depths, builds on love who teaches forgiveness.

My niece's feet are soft and clear.

Hamish Fulton's *no walk no work*.

1. GRØT:
THE LIMIT OF A YAWN
Caroline Bergvall

I don't know the name
of that steaming beige-looking porridge
strewn with a few peeled almonds
they sink a little into it
are swamped by it—
Being a thick white nameless
substance poured slowly
it slops formlessly
from the saucepan to the bowls
on the table—
Every year come christmas
it would insist—
Always something insists
that is known and felt
or perceived and not named
or named not—
Not unlike the wave
of a bioenergetic shiver
surprises the skin from the feet up
complements a train of thought
or surges it—
"In *My Pushkin*, Tsvetayeva says in passing:
it begins with a burning in the chest
and afterwards it is called love"—
Cixous writing this concludes:
"writing deploys itself *before*
'it is called'"—

There's the psychic thrust of physical syntax
the outer limit of the shell to the fruit
the inner limit of the fruit to the shell—
The limit of language in laughter
the limit of laughing to language
punctures the conversation increases blood flow—
The limit of the yawn to the jaw
is a cracked jaw
of a car crash to the spine
A thing collapses into action
the hard fact between two Cannot
be crossed until it is—
Clarifies their boundary
collapses into carSpine spineCrash
carRash carrash—
All week he's been dying
it takes her old father the greatest effort—
She sends distressed notes:
"death is a puking shitting agonising state for him
and still he breathes"—

SIMPLE PRESENT
Rodrigo Toscano

CREDIT Cut off—
"so
on your way!"
held
(were you?)

(in and around old '95)

The white luck of markets
deliberate odds

emptiness?

No universal luxuries
to poeticize here

Rationing then was for calm
Rationing now is for rage

ORGANIZATION

Gauntlets of indictments
to speak through
(did you?)

MEMORY what's missing
pressing
meaning
(little as a neutral concept)

They began with
what they had

was changing

Institutional Agreements
canceled
at the drop of a hat

the rate-of-profit hat
still falling ...

dragging with it
you too
activist

Began with clues
or rumors
of consensus

were accumulating

are dispersing

What person
couldn't sense force
aimed at their body
was likely ill

What person
couldn't free words

dictated by force
was likely ...

(here
in and around old '95
merely)
(and not so merely
did they falter)

WORDWORKERS
everyone

plugged
away

being taken

MEMORY

what's left
spend it
like there's no...

[sundried flower lit by the math of
by the smiling mock
by the penury
of our predicament
called

TOMORROW

AXIONOMETRIC MANHATTENINGS
Rodrigo Toscano

Somebody lost to endeavoring.

Jumped out in front.

Seriously unserious about it—everything.

Acute receptivity.

At the base of a scaffold elevator at the exterior of the beamwork perspective.

Site, terrifically gnarled spot-welding on the way up.

Beauty, achieved, leads to.

Aesthetic ideals.

Serious qualitative cloaca.

Somebody lost in endeavoring.

Somebody else rams smack into it.

That to the front (jumping) is to be more exposed than to the back (jumping).

Poetic practicality.

Unserious about core issues, a hyper-serious core heating up.

Lives that happen one by one that cling by two's and three's.

Rising vapor—entireties, over-valued, dissipate, just above the mezzanine.

Implicit complex of power positioning within a *realisum* of curves and angles.

City plan.

Leads to.

Four million uncoupled quotation marks scrambling about.

Serious quantitative cloaca.

Somebody on standby—fears idling down.

Somebody on standby—fears revving up.

Acute receptivity as punctual unconsciously knowing it, lending to the calculation *calculative* work.

How can (outside the bedrock of fact) somebody *lose* to endeavoring?

How can (outside a pile of facts—blasted) endeavoring *find* somebody to begin with?

At the top of the beamwork metaphor.

Hoisting down costly crooked calculations of political entropy.

Curiously stacked stockpiles of constructivist erotic surplus.

Metempsychosis.

"I am Lautréamont" the foreman reveals, "come back to—"

Somewhat too eager to—you'll notice.

Somewhat heinously unprepared to—*do it*—you'll notice *that*, drilling and/or welding, filing and/or mousing, schlepping and/or schtupping.

Second shift's assembling, first's on overtime, third's about to rise.

Somebody not somebody as yet, yet nobody's nobody.

How's it that 'endeavoring' is to be 'lost'—is an urban mystery.

What in the garrulous steely grid is he talking about?

Volitionary inklings, sparking burs by the billion, hot to the touch fractalled emotions.

Backwarping futurity.

PROLOGUE
Kaia Sand

1.
how to live in the galore
as we pack
purses

feed
ourselves each day

stopgap
the ratholes—
protect the patio garden

how to stretch a bungee
stretch and stretch it
fling it free
and damaging, timing
everything right

we're all bingeing—
united nations be damned;
we need a new sofa

how to pledge more rising
free and damaging
in this field of human
adjustments

2.
though we
thrive while
trodden, vowing
for vigor, no scorn
for longshots—

we are protractedly
worn

and on and on
and now like ourselves
occasionally, wrung thin
as meted urbane
promise, but
we can be exceptional
exceptional
as water is

we are the whereas, nimbly
the *nines*, cognitive
dissidents, and everyone
is seditious

THE PRESIDENT PROBABLY TALKS
Kaia Sand

the president probably talks to someone every day

sometimes his lips are moving, but our volume's too low

sometimes his voice is a tenth the volume of mine

sometimes his voice trembles inside my ten voices

sometimes his ten words devalue the currency

sometimes we promise

sometimes someone looks into someone's eyes for truth

sometimes we think we see it

in someone's ten coughs, tuberculosis is passed from cot to cot

sometimes ten walls separate me from two people making one decision

somewhere somehow ten women join ten women join ten women and march

my ten voices are still talking

somewhere in this city, ten meals in ten days is a boon

sometimes senators dine together

sometimes ten layoffs boom the business

sometimes we promise our poor

sometimes I feel like a holy-ten-voice-roller

in some sudden kiss, courage intensifies ten-fold

sometimes ten men join ten women join tens and tens and tens

sometimes someone somewhere somehow hears this

8

ATSURO RILEY

↓

KAY RYAN

↓

SARAH LINDSAY

↓

PATTIANN ROGERS

↓

JANE HIRSHFIELD

PICTURE
Atsuro Riley

This is the house (and jungle-strangled yard) I come from and carry.

The air out here is supper-singed (and bruise-tingeing) and close.

From where I'm hid (a perfect Y-crotch perch of medicine-smelling sweet-gum), I can belly-worry this (welted) branch and watch for swells (and coming squalls) along our elbow-curve of river, or I can hunker-turn and brace my trunk and limbs —and face my home.

Our roof is crimp-ribbed (and buckling) tin, and tar.

Our (in-warped) wooden porch-door is kick-scarred and splintering. The hinges of it rust-cry and -rasp in time with every Tailspin-wind, and jamb-slap (and after-slap), and shudder.

Our steps are slabs of cinder-crush and -temper, tamped and cooled.

See that funnel-blur of color in the red-gold glass? —Mama, mainly: boiling jelly. She's the apron-yellow (rickracked) plaid in there, and stove-coil coral; the quick silver blade-flash, plus the (magma-brimming) ladle-splash; that's her behind the bramble-berry purple, sieved and stored.

Out here, crickets are cricking their legs. Turtlets are cringing in their bunker-shells and burrows. Once-bedded nightcrawling worms are nerving up through beanvine-roots (and moonvines), —and dew-shining now, and cursive:

Mama will pressure-cook and scald and pan-scorch and frizzle.

Daddy will river-drift down to the (falling-down) dock.

I myself will monkey-shinny so high no bark-burns (or tree-rats, or tides)
*   or lava-spit can reach me.*

I will hunt for after-scraps (and sparks) and eat them all.

THE BELL
Atsuro Riley

The heard-tell *how her baby'd burned* downrivering and rippling.

Rill and wave of chicken prayer purlow murmuring back.

Brackwater cove-woods by her marsh-yard oak-creaking and -crying.

Mourn-cranes and eave-crow and crape-blinded windows keening black.

Raining; wrack.

The grieve-mother *Malindy Jean* porch-planking brunt and planging.

Breasting river (crossing-over) songs with cast-iron inside 'em.

The live heft-fact scorch-skillet willow-strung low and hanging.

Her heaving shovel-hafts and oars to make it ring.

IDEAL AUDIENCE
Kay Ryan

Not scattered legions,
not a dozen from
a single region
for whom accent
matters, not a seven-
member coven,
not five shirttail
cousins; just
one free citizen—
maybe not alive
now even—who
will know with
exquisite gloom
that only we two
ever found this room.

DOGLEG
Kay Ryan

Birds' legs
do of course
all dogleg
giving them
that bounce.
But these are
not normal odds
around the house.
Only two of
the dog's legs
dogleg and
two of the cat's.
Fifty-fifty: that's
as bad as it
gets usually,
despite the
fear you feel
when life has
angled brutally.

CHEESE PENGUIN
Sarah Lindsay

The world is large and full of ice;
it is hard to amaze. Its attention
may take the form of sea leopards.
That much any penguin knows
that staggers onto Cape Royds in the spring.
They bark, they bow one to another,
she swans forward, he walks on her back,
they get on with it. Later
he assumes his post, an egg between his ankles.

Explorers want to see everything, even
the faces of penguins whose eggs have been stolen
for science. At night they close the tent flaps
to fabricate sundown, hunch together
over penguin fried in butter, and write up their notes.
Mornings they clump over shit-stained rocks,
tuck eggs in their mittens, and shout.
Got one, got one. They shove back their balaclavas;
they feel warm all over.

The penguins scurry for something to mother,
anyone's egg will do, any egg
no matter how stiff and useless the contents,
even an egg-shaped stone to warm—
and one observer slips to a widow
a red tin that once held cheese.
Finally the wooden ship sails, full of salted penguin,

dozens of notebooks, embryos,
explorers who missed as little as possible. But:

The penguin cherished the red tin on her feet.
She knew what was meant to happen next
and she wanted it, with a pure desire
refined for thirty-five million years
in the dark eye of every progenitive cell.
And it happened. A red tin beak broke through
and a baby flopped into the rock nest, smelling of cheese—
but soon he was covered with guano, so that was all right.
Begging for krill from his aunts' throats just like the others.

Winter: blue ice, green ice, black sea,
hot breath of yellow-jawed killer whales.
Summer: pink slime on black rock,
skuas that aim for the eye. Krill, krill,
a shivering molt, krill, krill, a mate,
and so on. And though he craved dairy products
he never found any; though he was miraculous
no one came to say so. The world is large,
and without a fuss has absorbed stranger things than this.

VALHALLA BURN UNIT ON THE MOON CALLISTO

Sarah Lindsay

When Jupiter shields Valhalla impact basin
from the light of the small white sun
    and the streaming particles of its wind,
the patients who are able may come
    and linger in the courtyard,
with its soothing views of a thoroughly fireproof world—
concentric rings and ridges of ice and stone
    to the black horizon.
The patients move with exquisite care,
    never too close to each other or anything,
sipping bottled oxygen,
dressed, where they can be covered, in white
    cotton shifts and strips of gauze.
Even those with eyebrows and lashes
    appear to have two holes burned in their faces.
The doctors who watch them are not old,
    but their faces are slack and soft as worn denim.
Each qualified for this post by the loss
    of an irreplaceable love;
they aren't homesick for an Earth they could ever go back to.
There's room in them now for oceans of understanding,
and they see the use for severe burn victims
    of these conditions—
feeble light, mild gravity, ice-covered ground,
no touch of air to dread.
No atmosphere. That's why the sky is black
    all day, which does tend to bother the nurses,

the aides, the kitchen staff, the housekeeping crew,
   all of whom are encouraged to miss their planet
and, when they cry, are to do so hunched
   over sterile vials meant to preserve
the healing proteins found in common tears.

A COMMON SIGHT
Pattiann Rogers

There is at least one eye
for everything here this afternoon.
The algae and the yeasts, invisible
to some, for instance, are seen
by the protozoa; and the black-tailed
seeds of tadpoles are recognized
on sight by the giant, egg-carrying
water beetle. Brook trout have eyes
for caddisfly larvae, pickerel
for dragonfly nymphs; redfin shiners
bear witness to the presence
of flocks of water fleas.

The grains of the goldenrod
are valued, sought out, found
by the red-legged grasshopper who is,
in turn, noticed immediately
by the short-tailed shrew whose least
flitter alarms and attracts
the rodent-scoped eye
of the white-winged hawk.

There is an eye for everything.
The two-lined salamander watches
for the horsehair worm, as the stilt spider
pays sharp attention to midge fly,
crane fly. The cricket frog
will not pass unnoticed, being spied

specifically by the ringed raccoon,
and, despite the night beneath
the field, the earthworm, the grub
and the leafhopper larva are perceived
by the star-nosed mole.

So odd, that nothing goes unnoticed.
Even time has its testimony,
each copepod in the colony possessing
a red eyespot sensitive to the hour,
the entire congregation rising
as one body at dusk to touch the dark
where it exists above the pond.

And I have an eye myself
for this particular vision, this continuous
validation-by-sight that's given
and taken over and over by clam shrimp,
marsh treader, bob cat, the clover-coveting
honeybee, by diving teal, the thousand-eyed
bot fly, the wild and vigilant,
shadow-seeking mollusk mya.

Watch now, for my sake, how I stalk. Watch
how I secure this vision. Watch how long
and lovingly, watch
how I feed.

IN ADDITION TO FAITH, HOPE AND CHARITY
Pattiann Rogers

I'm sure there's a god
in favor of drums. Consider
their pervasiveness—the thump,
thump and slide of waves
on a stretched hide of beach,
the rising beat and slap
of their crests against shore
baffles, the rapping of otters
cracking molluscs with stones,
woodpeckers beak-banging, the beaver's
whack of his tail-paddle, the ape
playing the bam of his own chest,
the million tickering rolls
of rain off the flat-leaves
and razor-rims of the forest.

And we know the noise
of our own inventions—snare and kettle,
bongo, conga, big bass, toy tin,
timbales, tambourine, tom-tom.

But the heart must be the most
pervasive drum of all. Imagine
hearing all together every tinny
snare of every heartbeat
in every jumping mouse and harvest
mouse, sagebrush vole and least

shrew living across the prairie;
and add to that cacophony the individual
staccato tickings inside all gnatcatchers,
kingbirds, kestrels, rock doves, pine
warblers crossing, criss-crossing
each other in the sky, the sound
of their beatings overlapping
with the singular hammerings
of the hearts of cougar, coyote,
weasel, badger, pronghorn, the ponderous
bass of the black bear; and on deserts too,
all the knackings, the flutterings
inside wart snakes, whiptails, racers
and sidewinders, earless lizards, cactus
owls; plus the clamors undersea, slow
booming in the breasts of beluga
and bowhead, uniform rappings
in a passing school of cod or bib,
the thidderings of bat rays and needlefish.

Imagine the earth carrying this continuous
din, this multifarious festival of pulsing
thuds, stutters and drummings, wheeling
on and on across the universe.

This must be proof of a power existing
somewhere definitely in favor
of such a racket.

EACH MOMENT A WHITE BULL STEPS SHINING INTO THE WORLD
Jane Hirshfield

If the gods bring to you
a strange and frightening creature,
accept the gift
as if it were one you had chosen.

Say the accustomed prayers,
oil the hooves well,
caress the small ears with praise.

Have the new halter of woven silver
embedded with jewels.
Spare no expense, pay what is asked,
when a gift arrives from the sea.

Treat it as you yourself
would be treated,
brought speechless and naked
into the court of a king.

And when the request finally comes,
do not hesitate even an instant—

Stroke the white throat,
the heavy, trembling dewlaps
you'd come to believe were yours,
and plunge in the knife.

Not once
did you enter the pasture
without pause,
without yourself trembling.
That you came to love it, that was the gift.

Let the envious gods take back what they can.

THEOLOGY
Jane Hirshfield

If the flies did not hurry themselves to the window
they'd still die somewhere.

Other creatures choose the other dimension:
                                        to slip
into a thicket, swim into the shaded, undercut
part of the stream.

                        My dog would make her tennis ball
disappear into just such a hollow,
pushing it under the water with both paws.
Then dig for it furiously, wildly, until it popped up again.

A game or a theology, I could not tell.

The flies might well prefer the dawn-ribboned mouth of a trout,
its crisp and speed,
                        if they could get there,
though they are not in truth that kind of fly
and preference is not given often in these matters.

A border collie's preference is to do anything entirely,
with the whole attention. This Simone Weil called prayer.
And almost always, her prayers were successful—
                                        the tennis ball
could be summoned again to the surface.

When a friend's new pound dog, diagnosed distempered,

doctored for weeks, crawled under the porch to die, my friend
    crawled after,
pulled her out, said "No!",

as if to live were just a simple matter of training.
                          The coy-dog, startled, obeyed.
Now trots out to greet my car when I come to visit.

Only a firefly's evening blinking outside the window,
this miraculous story, but everyone hurries to believe it.

9

C.D. WRIGHT

↓

BRENDA HILLMAN

↓

HARRYETTE MULLEN

↓

ELIZABETH ALEXANDER

↓

FORREST HAMER

THIS COUPLE
C. D. Wright

Now is when we love to sit before mirrors
with a dark beer or hand out leaflets
at chainlink gates or come together after work
listening to each other's hard day. The engine dies,
no one hurries to go in. We might
walk around in the yard not making a plan.
The freeway is heard but there's no stopping
progress, and the week has barely begun. Then
we are dressed. It rains. Our heads rest
against the elevator wall inhaling a stranger;
we think of cliffs we went off
with our laughing friends. The faces
we put our lips to. Our wonderful sex
under whatever we wear. And of the car
burning on the side of the highway. Of jukeboxes
we fed. Quarters circulating with our prints.
Things we sent away for. Long drives. The rain. Cafes
where we ate late and once only. Eyes of an animal
in the headlamps. The guestbooks that verify
our whereabouts. Your apple core in the ashtray.
The pay toilets where we sat without paper. Rain.
Articles left with former lovers. The famous
ravine of childhood. Movie lines we've stood in
when it really came down. Moments
we have felt forsaken: waiting for the others
to step from the wrought iron compartment,
or passing through some town with the dial
on a Mexican station, wondering for the life of us,
where are we going and when would we meet.

FLOATING TREES
C. D. Wright

a bed is left open to a mirror
a mirror gazes long and hard at a bed

light fingers the house with its own acoustics

one of them writes this down
one has paper

bed of swollen creeks and theories and coils
bed of eyes and leaky pens

much of the night the air touches arms
arms extend themselves to air

their torsos turning toward a roll
of sound: thunder

night of coon scat and vandalized headstones
night of deep kisses and catamenia

his face by this light: saurian
hers: ash like the tissue of a hornets' nest

one scans the aisle of firs
the faint blue line of them
one looks out: sans serif

"Didn't I hear you tell them you were born
on a train"

what begins with a sough and ends with a groan
groan in which the tongue's true color is revealed

the comb's sough and the denim's undeniable rub
the chair's stripped back and muddied rung

color of stone soup and garden gloves
color of meal and treacle and sphagnum

hangers clinging to their coat
a soft-white bulb to its string

the footprints inside us
iterate the footprints outside

the scratched words return to their sleeves

the dresses of monday through friday
swallow the long hips of weekends

a face is studied like a key
for the mystery of what it once opened

"I didn't mean to wake you
angel brains"

ink of eyes and veins and phonemes
the ink completes the feeling

a mirror silently facing a door
door with no lock no lock

the room he brings into you
the room befalls you

like the fir trees he trues her
she nears him like the firs

if one vanishes one stays
if one stays the other will or will not vanish

otherwise my beautiful green fly
otherwise not a leaf stirs

CLOUDS NEAR SAN LEANDRO
Brenda Hillman

I.

The crack in social justice widened;
we saw the sparkle shelf below;

there had been some fragile delays
in back of the noetic cities,

berries on the blood ledge, sun-
lords with their seeds of steel,

snakes winding in the hungry age.
In the middle of our life

the dark woods had been clear-cut;
furies changed to quires of orange,

in spring, pelicans seen flying hillward,
their beaks like cut-up credit cards.

II.

In the middle of your life
you cast aside the brittle flame;

the doctor took some cancer off,
pain ceased to be an organizer.

Hadn't you preferred Nefertiti's blank left

eye to the rest? shape of
seeds the blue jays love, white

as the dream-egg heart of a
6 the courtier used for calling

other courtiers with his thumb—

III.
We're done with the old ironies,
is the thing of it. Some

foolish soul has sold his entire
Liz Phair collection back to Amoeba.

Used jewel cases seem almost tender,
gnostic smothered to smithereens-type plastic like

the mythic selves in Nietzsche, comet
making a comeback, the endless sheen—

IV.
So shake off the iron shoes
of fame and image and sing

near the dumb branch. Or enter
the pond where the angles swam.

Aren't there visions involving everything?
Some animals are warm in paradise;

your little alchemical salamander *taricha tarosa*
fresh from the being cycles stumbles

over rocks in its lyric outfit—

WIND TREATIES
Brenda Hillman

Between church bells
I held its breath:
air coming from half-states
it has visited where
dread meets ecstasy's skidmark.
Allow us, mighty and
bruised oxygen. And I
imagined a black square
made of ariadne-thread
around the great city,
winds coming from corners
such that talking would
never cease. Talking should
never cease, heads bent
over documents allowing distinction
or zhivagoing solitudes, stitches
at the edges of
dignity. Decades of give-it-away
while these winds worked.
Lamps flickering in the
stable districts. Symbolic weight
being added to bodies
walking in ordinary courtship
outfits, in a park.

SLEEPING WITH THE DICTIONARY
Harryette Mullen

I beg to dicker with my silver-tongued companion, whose lips are
ready to read my shining gloss. A versatile partner, conversant and
well-versed in the verbal art, the dictionary is not averse to the soli-
tary habits of the curiously wide-awake reader. In the dark night's
insomnia, the book is a stimulating sedative, awakening my tired
imagination to the hypnagogic trance of language. Retiring to the
canopy of the bedroom, turning on the bedside light, taking the big
dictionary to bed, clutching the unabridged bulk, heavy with the
weight of all the meanings between these covers, smoothing the thin
sheets, thick with accented syllables—all are exercises in the con-
scious regimen of dreamers, who toss words on their tongues while
turning illuminated pages. To go through all these motions and pro-
cedures, groping in the dark for an alluring word, is the poet's noc-
turnal mission. Aroused by myriad possibilities, we try out the most
perverse positions in the practice of our nightly act, the penetration of
the denotative body of the work. Any exit from the logic of language
might be an entry in a symptomatic dictionary. The alphabetical
order of this ample block of knowledge might render a dense lexicon
of lucid hallucinations. Beside the bed, a pad lies open to record the
meandering of migratory words. In the rapid eye movement of the
poet's night vision, this dictum can be decoded, like the secret acrostic
of a lover's name.

LAND OF THE DISCOUNT PRICE, HOME OF THE BRAND NAME
Harryette Mullen

My large magnetic car flag proudly displays Old Glory
as I drive to Family Dollar for the makings of a Fourth of July picnic.

I pledge allegiance to my MasterCard
that is honored in more stores than American Express.

Oh beautiful, those spacious aisles stacked high with seasonal items!

My country, 'tis of thee, sweet land of Lipton instant ice tea!

I've clipped a terrific recipe from Sunday's paper. A Betsy Ross
rectangular cake covered with strawberries, blueberries, and
Cool Whip,
with a coupon for the Cool Whip.

On Independence Day, our all-American front porch shows our
true colors
with patriotic bunting and bows, only $3.99 a yard (reg. $4.99).

Our backyard guests relax at our holiday picnic table,
thematically decorated with 10 oz. Stars and Stripes plastic tumblers,
matching table runner, paper plates and napkins from Dixie.

As my hubby grills the red meat and toasts the white buns under a
blue sky,
our son shows the neighbor kids his World Peacekeepers
Patriot Soldier,

a twelve-inch fully posable action figure that plays the national anthem.

LITTLE SLAVE NARRATIVE #1: MASTER
Elizabeth Alexander

He would order the women to pull up their clothes
"in Alabama style," as he called it. He would whip them

for not complying. He taught bloodhounds
to chase down negro boys, hence the expression

"hell-hounds on my trail." He was fond of peach brandy,
put ads in the paper: *Search high, search low*

for my runaway Isaac, my runaway Joe,
his right cheek scarred, occasioned by buckshot,

runaway Ben Fox, very black, chunky made,
two hundred dollars live, and if dead,

bring his dead body, so I may look at it.

THE DREAM THAT I TOLD
MY MOTHER-IN-LAW
Elizabeth Alexander

In the room almost filled with our bed,
the small bedroom, the king-sized bed high up
and on casters so sometimes we would roll,
in the room in the corner of the corner
apartment on top of a hill so the bed would roll,
we felt as if we might break off and drift,
float, and become our own continent.
When your mother first entered our apartment
she went straight to that room and libated our bed
with water from your homeland. Soon she saw
in my cheeks the fire and poppy stain,
and soon thereafter on that bed came the boy.
Then months, then the morning I cracked first one
then two then three eggs in a white bowl
and all had double yolks, and your mother
(now our mother) read the signs. Signs everywhere,
signs rampant, a season of signs and a vial
of white dirt brought across three continents
to the enormous white bed that rolled
and now held three, and soon held four,
four on the bed, two boys, one man, and me,
our mother reading all signs and blessing our bed,
blessing our bed filled with babies, blessing our bed
through her frailty, blessing us and our bed,
blessing us and our bed.

                        She began to dream
of childhood flowers, her long-gone parents.
I told her my dream in a waiting room:
A photographer photographed women,
said her portraits revealed their truest selves.
She snapped my picture, peeled back the paper,
and there was my son's face, my first son, my self.
Mamma loved that dream so I told it again.

And soon she crossed over to her parents,
sisters, one son (War took that son.
We destroy one another), and women came
by twos and tens wrapped in her same fine white
bearing huge pans of stew, round breads, homemade wines,
and men came in suits with their ravaged faces
and together they cried and cried and cried
and keened and cried and the sound
was a live hive swelling and growing,
all the water in the world, all the salt, all the wails,
and the sound grew too big for the building and finally
lifted what needed to be lifted from the casket and we quieted
and watched it waft up and away like feather, like ash.
Daughter, she said, when her journey began, *You are a mother now,*
and you have to take care of the world.

TWELVE
Forrest Hamer

And my grandfather was dead for just months, and the family was
unmooring, his children now the elders among us, some of them
living far away.

And my father had returned to Viet Nam for another year, and this
time he volunteered which made no real sense to me, the way his
rules made no sense but he was leaving them behind, anyway.

And my mother was without the men she loved, and I was a boy.

And the man I looked to to take my father's place drank to the point
of being a drunk, but he liked me and he liked that I liked him, even
if the liking he wanted was not the liking I felt.

And I grew what looked like a foot of inches, suddenly, my body
reaching at its final height.

And Martin Luther King was murdered, and the town instantly set
a curfew, and everyone in the North End stayed inside, all fury and
despairing eager to find the way out.

And the Emancipation Proclamation was what people kept talking
about, as if words by themselves could describe that freedom.

And Master Woodard told him he could stay on the plantation and
become one of their farming assistants.

And from the playground the sixth-graders had all to ourselves, we
watched the marchers carrying tall signs, the woman with the deep

voice looking straight at me and saying, We're causing this trouble for *you.*

And he left his master, glad, wondering would he want to remember, and who ever would remember him in the far from now.

And I lost interest in any history but becoming 13.

And there was a freedom I could imagine.

And my best friend was my cousin Larry, who was my age and kept secrets.

And the boys just older formed a group we could belong to if we passed one at a time through their gauntlet.

And the 14 children who would be born and who would die waited for him to leave sharecropping, meet Jemima Thompson and become the man who is their father.

And he would tell himself as Benjamin Barnes, born in 18 and 53, who had been called already to be a preacher.

And he tended beans, cotton, corn, and peanuts.

And for the first time I cropped tobacco, cropped for four days, the misery of which I would not tell excepting my cousin and my brother and my aunt.

And his friend from the plantation was Willie; they laughed with each other about things, and he promised he would name a son the name of his friend.

And he loved the sound of his freedom, and he sang it often.

And in my bed I felt myself burning between the pajamas and my stomach, and it was a new happiness.

And I began not liking church music, wanting instead to dance on Sundays, especially the Boogaloo.

And I wanted my father's permission by mail to get a Quo Vadis haircut, promising now I would take care of my hair.

And he began thinking someday he could marry.

And my cousin and I debated the meanings of soul, and wondered when our people would become free.

And those of us afraid of snakes were sent each to capture one and to care for it, and those of us afraid of heights were sent to the roof of the North End School to stand at the ledge and to look.

And I asked to keep my Papa Willie's pocket watch, the one with the second hand bent and the crystal chipped.

And he began making long walks, farther away and back.

And he figured the world laid before him good, anyway, despite the stark hatreds.

And he thought all the days and nights of that year only of freedom.

A POEM ALSO ABOUT WHITENESS
Forrest Hamer

I have never dreamed of being white. In my dreams I have always been black as much as I can see, though sometimes my parents are not black. One night I was taking care of my parents who were old and white; they were as familiar to me as parents are in dreams, and it wasn't until I was awake I noticed I've never met these particular people. I hope they are well.

A man I know dreams himself sometimes as Asian and he asks if I think dreams are expressions of wishes; I ask him to suppose this is true, and he doubts it. The next night I am a white woman granting him six wishes though all he ever wishes for is time. He misses the Mexican housekeeper he had growing up; since knowing me he thinks about her more than he has in years. What do I think of this, he asks.

A woman who is black and white sometimes dreams of herself as white and sometimes as black, and she is never both things in her dreams. She thinks this happens because she is always choosing one parent or the other, blown back and forth between them like an oak leaf in late November. Her skin is the color of amber, but in her dreams she is a woman the color of teak or a woman the color of milk.

I have to admit I have wished at times to be white. Usually, I am colored and awake, imagining myself invisible.

10

DEAN YOUNG

↓

MARY RUEFLE

↓

RALPH ANGEL

↓

ÁNGEL GARCÍA

↓

GERRY LAFEMINA

RABBIT, I LOVE YOU
Dean Young

The capacity to feel is good to have,
you know you are alive when
you feel the ravine's minuet
of sadness, the octopus' gladness
at being in the sea and not a jelly jar.
Having feelings allows us to do nothing
but still feel something is getting done.
Many thinkers know the feeling
of the feeling but few have glimpsed
the feeling of the feeling of the feeling.
The rabbit does not move, waiting
for the yard to turn rabbit-colored
and thus make it feel invisible. Huh?
You can argue for hours about a rabbit
if the feeling is there which is often
not about the rabbit but the person
you argue with, her hair tied
to a river, her unstable tongue.
Such heat in the world you
and the rabbit share. And cold,
demurs the glacier. You lock your keys
in the car and there's a feeling waiting.
Read Nick Caraway's last words and yep,
a feeling. There are no ordinary feelings
just as there are no ordinary spring days
or kicked-over cans of paint. Are
feelings ever succinct? The haiku is quick .
but its ripples to the horizon go.

Feeling—you think you have it
under control then wham-o, a new
blast hole in the middle of the couch
where you're tv-watching some excessively
handsome people try to defuse an atomic bomb
and now your throat is shaking.
Tears! Even for the toddler, feeling
is a thousand years old just as the smile
of Mona Lisa is new every 15 minutes.
You've got to be kidding. Matter, anti-
matter, there's still a lot unaccounted for.
Feeling, you'll never stop bush-whacking me
unsyntactically like crows flying from a tree.
Even in sleep, dreamily I leap
from the top stair to grab the arrow
about to pierce my father's chest.
I saved him I think for a moment
then the feeling, no, that isn't so.

HOW I GET MY IDEAS
Dean Young

Sometimes you just have to wait
15 seconds then beat the prevailing nuance
from the air. If that doesn't work,
try to remember how many times
you've wakened in the body of an animal,
two arms, two legs, willowy antennae.
Try thinking what it would be like
to never see your dearest again.
Stroke her gloves, sniff his overcoat.
If that's a no-go, call Joe
who's never home but keeps changing
the melody of his message.
Cactus at night emits its own light,
the river flows under the sea.
Dear face I always recognize but never
know, everything has a purpose
from which it must be freed,
maybe with crowbars, maybe the gentlest breeze.
Always turn in the direction of the skid.
If it's raining, use the rain
to lash the windowpanes or,
in a calmer mode, deepen the new greens
nearly to a violet. I can't live
without violet although it's red
I most often resort to.
Sometimes people become angelic when they cry,
sometimes only ravaged.
Technically, Mary still owes me a letter,

her last was just porcupine quills and tears,
tears that left a whitish residue
on black construction paper.
Sometimes I look at used art books at Moe's
just to see women without their clothes.
How can someone so rich,
who can have fish whenever he wants,
go to baseball games,
still feel such desperation?
I'm afraid I must insist
on desperation. By the fourth week
the embryo has nearly turned itself
inside out. If that doesn't help,
you'll just have to wait which
may involve sleeping which may involve
dreaming and sometimes dreaming works.
Father, why have you returned,
dirt on your morning vest?
You cannot control your laughter.
You cannot control your love.
You know not to hit the brakes on ice
but do anyway. You bend the nail
but keep hammering because
hammering makes the world.

TALKING TO STRANGERS
Mary Ruefle

Do you see sun spots? A strong, terrible love where
there isn't any? A demoiselle crane talking to a lama
duck? Very interesting, but there's nothing in it.
Some people take electric roses and plant them in a field
to bring the field down to earth.
There's nothing wrong with that. Put down your book.
Look at me when I talk to you. I'm the oxygen mask
that comes dangling down in a plane.
I'm here to help you be garrulous.
I'm not interested in your family—not your mother,
father, brother, sister, son, daughter, lover or
dog. In France, they used to kill themselves if
a dinner party went wrong. That's a great idea.
Are you interested in orphan-types who turn out
to be kings, or kings who come to nothing?
What's the difference between watching and looking?
Doff your garb. I'm sorry, but the loggerhead turtles
off the Carolina coast are leaving for Africa tonight.
Would you like an ice cold pear instead?
Walking into the store is like entering
the delicate refrain of a Christmas poem.
What more could you want? Siddhartha said
someone who brushes against you in the street
has shared an experience with you for five hundred lives.
Can bottles bobbing on the open sea
be said to move at all?

FASTER LOVE IS ALL THERE IS
Mary Ruefle

There is nothing faster than more faster love
faster love is all there is
as it is 4:03 and life takes another
amazing and distressful turn
as when a sea gull
picks up a French fry
and becomes human

What are we to do at sea
with our logarithms
when faster love is all there is

When April has forty-six days
after which it can't go on
floating on the mattress
so it rises so we can see
the flowers it was once upon
and a few strands of brownish hair

When we tip toe down the hall for ice
When ice falls out of the shoot and into the bucket
When a cube falls through the grate and is gone

When we huddle in our sea of cars
When we suffer muchly from glare in the face
and keep the eyes alive
with nothing more than an eyedropper

When we never went snorkeling
but nonetheless sensed people
are more capable of floating by
than any other creature

Stop stop pretty water
Raise a cup of kindness to them
As it is there's nothing faster
Faster love, it's all there is

THE HEART OF THINGS
Ralph Angel

And so say nothing of the birds
out back, or how the leaves of trees grow louder
than the city, how a room
begins again as though it had been taken away
only. Whatever now
that I'm afraid of, but casually, like someone
sitting crosswise in her chair, her legs
curved over one side, sipping a glass of wine
and spying on her neighbors,
not ill-arranged things really, but that sense
of realism that takes up a lot more time
than I or anyone together
has to give.

And so stayed longer, he said, into the evening
behind the page and out of the cold,
even the dead are free again
to love us as in life a human being
is singled out and standing there, on the curb,
shifting the way we do from
foot to shoeless foot,

and so broke
apart the vision I expected
of myself, confused among those
dozing on the platform, and at home the air
is moist again with tea, but
faintly so, those fragrant several moments

that sound the most like dream,
like dreaming aloud the nightmare
that I alone am still.

NOBODY'S DEAD THERE
Ralph Angel

The road sloped
mostly sideways. It's okay
that I'm sleepy. The moon on the lake
followed us home.
Today's rain is more tropical. No family
anywhere, or that sense
of cold.

It's important not to
yell at your neighbor. It's what she
wants you to do. I only hate
what I pity. I am a transitory and not too disgruntled
citizen of a city deemed
sleepless
for the sake of its very small
fishes. You are
my tongue.

We must attend to
and bless the amenities. We wash our hands
and go nuts. I know morning's
crazy. I know
bread.
A few slices were once
used as stepping stones. Thank God
for friends. I hear the thrush

repeating itself.
There's a prayer for that
too, remember?
We eat less and less. We run and we
exercise. The whole point is to open old wounds and
not talk.
Only then is the quiet
nothing more than the sound of the tires.
To this day, knock
on wood.

ON NIGHTS LIKE THESE
Ángel García

In a dimly lit bar where my face remains barely visible,
I could recount my entire life to no one, a story which
pours from my lips quicker than the time it takes to down
a beer, nothing left in my cold mug, afterward, except the quiet.
But tonight, I sit alone in a cluttered room, comforted by
a cold and sweating 40 ounce beer and a book of poems
whose words, worn down by my own touch, whisper
    who hasn't lodged in the belly of something?
      who hasn't been devoured?
and in my state, intoxicated by beer and verse, both lethal
before sleep, I want to believe the wind outside my thin windows
is a young child who finds the greatest pleasure in tickling
the soft underbellies of the leaves, making them cry out
something like the start of rain. This is not about precision.
No. But what occurs in the darkness, so deep, so thick
nothing else can breathe except the poet who demands,
unforgivingly, a little drunkenness, a little metaphor.
On nights like this it is easier to sit in the darkness,
drunk, scratching out lines crookedly across the page
than to notice how silence consumes when it is so still,
so suffocating you could actually hear it, when a man
chokes up the pain of a clenched fist against the wall,
of crucifixes carved, unwillingly, into the flesh of a forearm.

BEAUTY
Ángel García

I know the moon is disturbing,
to stand beneath the shower of its brilliance
and have absolutely nothing in your pocket
except maybe, pocket lint or the few pennies
you've managed to collect off the cold concrete,
hoping because they're *heads up* something
about your life might change irreversibly,
& how enough of those pennies might buy
you something, or nothing, an air-conditioned
bus ride into the next town where men and women
pass you by while pressing their coats against their bodies,
as if you were nothing more than a cold breeze,
how if you stood beneath the moon it might convince you
there's just not enough beauty in the world to go around.

POEM WITH THE MORNING SUN
REFLECTED IN FRESHLY SHINED SHOES
Gerry LaFemina

There's the wind pushing its invisible broom
& taxis filled with drunk tourists perusing emptying avenues.
The night like a book read a long time ago—
a fuzzy memory with a story line you could tell,

not precisely, but well enough to make your meaning plain.
A night like this

its belly full of wind & the wind
in the wake of those automobiles, one might find a sliver
of the absolute. A haze of skyline

beckons the eyes of a homeless man in the park
who nightly sleeps under the statue of a man on horseback
& dreams visions of being trampled to death

or riding away on a palomino from this place.

Each morning he wakes to joggers' footsteps
running the paths.

        *   *   *

In another life he drove a taxi.
In another life he read stories to his nephews
from the same book his mother read to him.

Some mornings when the sun's inky luminescence bleeds
along the eastern horizon, he thinks of his nephews
both of whom are nameless now.
& of his mother. & of a woman to whom he almost vowed his life.

She must rarely think of him these days
although sometimes, I imagine, someone at a nearby table
in a restaurant might say his name
referring, of course, to somebody else—a person enmeshed in
   the narrative

of a different biography—
& a stain will startle her cheeks. She'll excuse herself then,
quickly & without warning, to weep in the women's room
for a few brief seconds. She's tried explaining this

to her husband
tried telling the story, but now she doesn't even quite recall
the feel of his hands or the song he used to hum
in the car when he drove. She wouldn't know him

were she to see him,
although the way she might move her arm to tighten her grip
on her purse—this simple gesture—

might enable him
to recognize her or at least to recognize
how cold the wind is from the north

which means there is a wind
& a north & a world beyond the incidental.

*   *   *

What is madness if not

perception? He hears a voice in the wind singing
what was once their song; he believes the cooing of pigeons &
          how much

it sounds like the vibrating purr of a cat. He's amazed
by the old men who come out each morning to shine shoes as the
          halogen sun
just begins burning the city's grim epidermis: he sees them

kneeling at their labors hands gesticulating,
as if seeking benediction.

THE SILENCE THAT FOLLOWS
Gerry LaFemina

It's early summer in Grayling, & death has no business here
despite my neighbor celebrating his 93rd June.
Black flies convene above
                              the ruffled surface of the AuSable
while adolescents dream of canoeing toward Wakely Bridge
with dates or their fathers. On street corners

the stands are up, some selling cherry bombs & rockets,
some selling Old Mission cherries. I knew a young woman,
yes, years ago, who could twist
                              cherry stems into knots
with her tongue, & what young man wouldn't love that?
All I could do was spit the pits of those tart fruits

& never far enough to win a ribbon at Cherry Fest.
All I could do was tell her *I love you*, but
there was no ribbon for that, either.
                              Still, I'll stop my car
along the shoulder of West 72, buy a pound of cherries
& admire their merlot bodies, their skin

taut & rounded. I could be in love all over again
with the scent of fresh cherries. When it ended
there was nothing our tongues could do,
                              no words we might tie
together to make anything all right. Her name translates
into *I love* or *I like*. I lived three blocks from Mercy Hospital then

though there was no mercy to be had that long August
in the empty bag of our house. I sat & listened
to ambulances rushing in.

      The sirens howled like a lonely man
or like a lonely woman. It's early summer in Grayling,
& I have three dollars worth of cherries, & I never did learn

how she did that trick with her tongue & the stem,
though I used to finger those knots like a Persian
reading a rug. Translation's

      such a subjective art. I'd say
her name twice in a row—*I like I like*—
& now I've stopped saying it at all, & stopped even

thinking of her. Tonight I'll eat Michigan cherries from brown paper
& from my porch watch an ambulance hurry with its charges.
Behind it, a car full of prayers.

      In the silence that follows
I might hear the river only a block away:
a quick splashing of something crossing over to the near shore.

CONTRIBUTORS

ELIZABETH ALEXANDER is the author of four books of poems, most recently *American Sublime* (2003), and a collection of essays, *The Black Interior* (2004). She is a professor at Yale University and lives in New Haven, Connecticut.

RALPH ANGEL is the author of three collections of poetry: *Neither World* (1995), winner of the James Laughlin Award; *Anxious Latitudes* (1986); and most recently, *Twice Removed* (Sarabande Books, 2001). In October, Sarabande will publish a fourth collection, *Exceptions and Melancholies*, as well as his translation of Federico García Lorca's *Poem of the Deep Song*.

JOHN ASHBERY has published more than 20 collections of poetry, including, most recently, *Where Shall I Wander* (Ecco/HarperCollins [US] and Carcanet [UK], 2005). His *Selected Prose* was published in 2004 by Carcanet and The University of Michigan Press. Since 1990 he has been the Charles P. Stevenson, Jr. Professor of Languages and Literature at Bard College in Annandale-on-Hudson, New York.

CAROLINE BERGVALL is a poet and performance artist based in London, England. Books include: *Goan Atom* (Krupskaya, 2001) and *Eclat* (Sound&Language, 1996). Her most recent collection of poetic and performance pieces, *FIG (Goan Atom 2)* was recently published (Salt Books, 2005) and her CD of readings and audiotexts, *Via: poems 1994-2004 (Rockdrill 8)* is available through Carcanet. As an artist, she has developed text performances as well as collaborative pieces with sound artists, both in Europe and in North America. She is co-Chair of the MFA Writing Faculty, Milton Avery School of the Arts, Bard College (NY) and Research Fellow at Dartington College of Arts (Devon).

DAVID BERMAN was born in Williamsburg, Virginia, in 1967. He graduated from the Greenhill School in Addison, Texas, the University of Virginia, and the University of Massachusetts. His first book is *Actual Air* (Open City, 1999). Recent poems have appeared in *The Believer* and *Fence*. His band, the Silver Jews, has released five albums on Drag City Records: *The Natural Bridge, Starlite Walker, American Water, Bright Flight*, and *Tanglewood Numbers*. He lives in Nashville, Tennessee.

MICHAEL BURKARD's books include *My Secret Boat* (W. W. Norton, 1990), *Fictions from the Self* (Norton, 1988), *Unsleeping* (Sarabande Books, 2001) and *Pennsylvania Collection Agency* (New Issues Press, 2001). Poems appearing in upcoming issues of *APR* and *parakeet*. He teaches in the MFA Program in Creative Writing at Syracuse University.

TINA CHANG is the author of *Half-Lit Houses* (Four Way Books, 2004). Her poems have appeared in *American Poet, Indiana Review, The Missouri Review, Ploughshares, Quarterly West, Sonora Review*, among others. Her work has been anthologized in *Identity Lessons* (Penguin Putnam, 1999) *Poetry Nation* (Vehicule Press, 1998), *Asian American Literature* (McGraw-Hill, 2001), *Asian American Poetry: The Next Generation* (University of Illinois Press, 2004) and in *Poetry 30: Poets in Their Thirties* (MAMMOTH Books, 2005). She teaches at Sarah Lawrence College and Hunter College. She is co-editing an anthology of East Asian, South Asian, and Middle Eastern Poetry which is forthcoming from W. W. Norton & Co. (2007).

LYNN EMANUEL is the author of three books of poetry, *Hotel Fiesta* (University of Georgia Press, 1984), *The Dig* (University of Illinois Press, 1994), and *Then, Suddenly—* (University of Pittsburgh Press, 1999), which was awarded the Eric Matthieu King Award from The Academy of American Poets. Her work has been featured in the

Pushcart Prize Anthology and the *Best American Poetry* numerous times and was selected by Paul Muldoon for inclusion in the 2005 edition of *Best American.* "My Subjectivity:" is from a book in progress tentatively entitled *The War Years.*

OLENA KALYTIAK DAVIS is the author of two collections of poetry, *shattered sonnets love cards and other off and back handed importunites* (Tin House/Bloomsbury Press, 2003), a Spring 2004 Book Sense Poetry Top Ten Pick, and *And Her Soul Out Of Nothing* (University of Wisconsin Press, 1997), which was selected by Rita Dove for the Brittingham Prize in Poetry. Her poems have appeared in numerous journals and anthologies, including four *Best American Poetry* volumes, and have won a Pushcart Prize. The recipient of a Guggenheim Fellowship, a Rona Jaffe Foundation writers grant and several grants from the Alaska and Juneau Arts Councils, she writes and raises her two children in Anchorage, Alaska.

MARK DOTY's most recent book of poems is *School of the Arts* (HarperCollins, 2005). Next spring Harper will publish a new prose book, *Dog Years.* He teaches at the University of Houston every fall, and lives otherwise in New York City.

ÁNGEL GARCÍA recently graduated from the Creative Writing Program at the University of Redlands. In the fall he will be attending graduate school in pursuit of an MFA. He currently lives and writes in Long Beach.

FORREST HAMER is the author of *Call & Response* (1995); *Middle Ear* (2000), winner of the Bay Area Book Reviewers Association Award; and the forthcoming *Rift.*

FRANCINE J. HARRIS is a Cave Canem fellow who has been recently published in *Tribes, the Furnace* and has work appearing in the new

Cave Canem anthology *Gathering Ground*. Having lived in lots of big cities, she is at heart a small-town, Midwestern poet raised in and living in Detroit, where she teaches high school poetry.

TERRANCE HAYES is the author of *Wind in a Box* (Penguin, 2006), *Hip Logic* (Penguin, 2002) and *Muscular Music* (Carnegie Mellon University Press, 2005; Tia Chucha Press, 1999). His honors include a Whiting Writers Award, the Kate Tufts Discovery Award, a National Poetry Series award, a Pushcart Prize, a Best American Poetry selection, and a National Endowment for the Arts Fellowship. He lives in Pittsburgh, Pennsylvania.

BRENDA HILLMAN is the author of seven collections of poetry, the most recent of which is *Pieces of Air in the Epic* (Wesleyan UP, 2005). She teaches at Saint Mary's College is Moraga, California.

JANE HIRSHFIELD is the author of six collections of poetry, including the newly published *After* (HarperCollins, 2006) and *Given Sugar, Given Salt* (HarperCollins, 2001), a finalist for the National Book Critics Circle Award, and a collection of essays, *Nine Gates: Entering the Mind of Poetry* (HarperCollins, 1997). Her work has appeared in *The New Yorker, The Atlantic Monthly, The Nation, Poetry*, and *The Best American Poetry*, among other publications, and her honors include fellowships from the Guggenheim and Rockefeller Foundations, the National Endowment for the Arts, and the Academy of American Poets. Her books have appeared on bestseller lists in San Francisco, Detroit, Canberra, and Krakow.

DENIS JOHNSON is the author of seven novels; the short story collection *Jesus' Son* (1992); five plays; and five poetry collections, including *The Throne of the Third Heaven of the Nations Millennium General Assembly: Poems Collected and New* (1996). He has received many awards for his work, including a Lannan Fellowship in Fiction and a

Whiting Writer's Award. Johnson is currently playwright-in-residence at the Campo Santo theater company at San Francisco's Intersection for the Arts.

A. VAN JORDAN is the author of *Rise*, published by Tia Chucha Press in 2001, which won a 2002 Pen/Oakland Josephine Miles Award, and *M-A-C-N-O-L-I-A*, published by WW Norton Co. in 2004, for which he was awarded a 2004 Whiting Writers Award and an Anisfield-Wolf Book Award. He also received a Pushcart Prize in 2006. He teaches at the University of Texas at Austin.

Raised in Nashville, THOMAS KANE is an M.F.A. candidate in poetry at the University of Pittsburgh. His translations of Tomaž Šalamun's work are forthcoming in *Crazyhorse*.

MARY KARR's latest poems are published in *Sinners Welcome* by Harpers Collins (2006). She was a Guggenheim Fellow in poetry last year and is the Peck Professor of Literature at Syracuse University. She's published two bestselling memoirs, *The Liars' Club* (1995) and *Cherry* (2000). She's working on a third, *Lit*.

RUTH ELLEN KOCHER is the author of *One Girl Babylon* (2003), *When the Moon Knows You're Wandering* (2001), winner of the Green Rose Prize in Poetry; and *Desdemona's Fire* (1999), winner of the Naomi Long Madgett Poetry Award. Her work has appeared in various journals, including *Ploughshares, Crab Orchard Review, Clackamas Literary Review, The Missouri Review, African American Review, The Gettysburg Review,* and *Antioch,* among others.

YUSEF KOMUNYAKAA teaches creative writing at New York University. His latest book, *Gilgamesh* (a verse play), is forthcoming from Wesleyan University Press in October, 2006.

GERRY LAFEMINA is the author of five collections of poetry, including *The Parakeets of Brooklyn*, winner of the 2003 Bordighera Prize and published in a bilingual edition of Italian and English, and *The Window Facing Winter* (2004). He is also co-editor of the anthology *Poetry 30* (2005), featuring the work of thirty-something poets, and of the journal *Review Revue*, which features poetry reviews, interviews, and prosody essays. He teaches at Frostburg Sate University where he directs the Frostburg Center for Creative Writing.

PATRICK LAWLER has published three collections of poetry: *A Drowning Man is Never Tall Enough* (University of Georgia Press, 1990), *reading a burning book* (Basfal Books, 1994), and *Feeding the Fear of the Earth*, winner of the Many Mountains Moving poetry book competition and published in 2006. Mr. Lawler has been awarded fellowships by the New York State Foundation for the Arts, the National Endowment of the Arts, and the Constance Saltonstall Foundation for the Arts. An Associate Professor at SUNY College of Environmental Science and Forestry, he teaches Environmental Writing and Nature Literature. In addition, he teaches creative writing courses, including drama, for LeMoyne College and Onondaga Community College.

SARAH LINDSAY is the author of two books in the Grove Press Poetry Series: *Primate Behavior* (1997), a finalist for the National Book Award, and *Mount Clutter* (2002). She lives in Greensboro, North Carolina, and earns her keep as copy editor of several magazines and a catalogue at Pace Communications.

HARRYETTE MULLEN's poems, short stories, and essays have been published widely and reprinted in over 40 anthologies. Her poetry is included in the latest edition of the *Norton Anthology of African American Literature* (2004) and has been translated into Spanish, French, Polish, Bulgarian, and Swedish. She is the author of six poetry books, most recently *Blues Baby* (Bucknell University, 2002) and *Sleeping with the Dictionary* (University of California, 2002). The latter was a finalist for a National Book Award, National Book Critics Circle Award, and Los Angeles Times Book Prize. In 2004 she received a grant from the Foundation for Contemporary Arts and in 2005 she was awarded a fellowship from the John Simon Guggenheim Memorial Foundation. She was born in Alabama, grew up in Texas, and now lives in Los Angeles, where she teaches at UCLA. Her book *Recyclopedia* is forthcoming from Graywolf Press in 2006.

ALICE NOTLEY lives in Paris, France. She has two books of poetry scheduled for publication in 2006: *Grave of Light: Selected Poems 1970-2005* (Wesleyan) and *Alma, or The Dead Women* (Granary Books).

MICHAEL ONDAATJE is the author of four books of poetry, most recently *The Cinnamon Peeler* (1997), and *Handwriting* (1999). He has also written numerous books of criticism and fiction, including the Booker Prize-winning novel *The English Patient* (1992), and *Anil's Ghost* (2000). Born in Sri Lanka, Ondaatje lived to England between 1954 and 1962 before moving to Canada, where he has lived ever since.

LINDA TOMOL PENNISI's first book of poems, *Seamless*, won the 2003 Perugia Press Intro Prize, its publication supported by a Greenwald Fund Grant from the American Academy of Poets. *Suddenly, Fruit*, winner of the Carolina Wren Chapbook Prize, will be published in spring, 2006. A recipient of a Constance Saltonstall Individual Artists Grant, Pennisi has had poems appear in journals such as *Lyric Poetry Review*, *Runes* and *Hunger Mountain*. She presently directs the Creative Writing Program at Le Moyne College in Syracuse, N.Y.

HEIDI JOHANNESEN POON was born in 1966 and lives with her family in Charlottesville, Virginia.

COURTNEY QUEENEY's work appears in *Three New Poets* (Sheep Meadow Press, 2006). Her first collection, *Filibuster to Delay a Kiss and Other Poems*, is forthcoming from Random House in 2007. Thanks to Peter Mishler for the title "Eloping Alone."

ATSURO RILEY's work has appeared in *Poetry, The Threepenny Review,* and *The Pushcart Prize XXX.*

MARY RUEFLE is the author of nine books of poetry, most recently *A Little White Shadow* (Wave Books, 2006). She lives in Vermont.

KAY RYAN has written six books of poetry, most recently *The Niagara River* (Grove Press, 2005). A few years ago one of her poems, "Patience," showed up in the cartoon strip *Boondocks*. Huey quoted the second half of it, to Riley's utter disgust.

Canadian poet LISA ROBERTSON lives in France. A new book, *The Men,* has just been published by Bookthug, in Toronto. Past titles include *Debbie: an Epic* (1997), *The Weather* (2001), and *Occasional Works and Seven Walks from the Office for Soft Architecture* (2003).

PATTIANN ROGERS has published 12 books, most recently *Firekeeper, Selected Poems, Revised and Expanded Edition* (Milkweed, 2005) and *Generations* (Penguin, 2004). *Song of the World Becoming, New and Collected Poems, 1981–2001* (Milkweed, 2001) was a finalist for the LA Times Book Prize and an Editor's Choice from *Booklist*. Rogers is the recipient of a 2005 Literary Award for Poetry from the Lannan Foundation, two NEA Grants, and a Guggenheim Fellowship. Her poetry has won three prizes from *Poetry*, two from *Prairie Schooner*, two from *Poetry Northwest*, and five Pushcart Prizes. Her papers are archived at Texas Tech University. Rogers has taught as visiting professor at several universities and was an associate professor at the University of Arkansas. She is the mother of two sons, grandmother of three grandsons, and lives with her husband, a retired geophysicist, in Colorado.

KAIA SAND is the author of *interval* (Edge Books, 2004), and co-editor of the *Tangent*, a zine, chapbook series, and currently-dormant-but-archived radio program thetangentpress.org. Printer and book artist Ruth Lingen typeset Sand's text in a limited edition set of small books, 2005. Most recently, her poems can be found in *Tool a Magazine* <www.toolamagazine.com>, *Ixnay Reader*, the *Cambridge Poetry Summit 2005* anthology, *Tinfish Net*, *Dusie* <www.dusie.org>, and *Primary Writing*. She lives in Portland, Oregon.

TRACY K. SMITH teaches in the Creative Writing Program at Princeton University. She is the recipient of awards from the Ludwig Vogelstein, Rona Jaffe and Mrs. Giles Whiting Foundations. Her collection of poems, *The Body's Question* (Graywolf Press), won the 2002 Cave Canem Poetry Prize.

MARY STEBBINS has an MFA in Creative Writing in Poetry from Vermont College. She taught *Creative Writing* at LeMoyne College and *Nature and the Creative Writer* and *The Literature of Nature* at SUNY College of Environmental Science and Forestry and at Beaver Lake Nature Center. Her latest poems have been published in *Avocet, edificeWrecked* and *The Bitter Oleander*.

LARISSA SZPORLUK is the author of *Dark Sky Question* (1998); *Isolato* (2000); *The Wind, Master Cherry, the Wind* (2003); and the forthcoming *Embryos and Idiots*. She is an associate professor of English at Bowling Green State University.

JAMES TATE won the Pulitzer Prize in 1991 for his *Selected Poems,* and the National Book Award in 1994 for *Worshipful Company of Fletchers.* He teaches at the University of Massachusetts.

RODRIGO TOSCANO is the author of *To Leveling Swerve* (Krupskaya Books, 2004), *Platform* (Atelos, 2003), *The Disparities* (Green Integer, 2002) and *Partisans* (O Book, 1999). He was a New York State Foundation for the Arts 2005 Fellow in Poetry and appeared in *Best American Poetry 2004* (Scribners). His writing and has been translated into French, German, Spanish, Italian, and Serbo-Croatian. Originally from California, Toscano has been living in NYC for the last seven years, where he works at the Labor Institute.

BRETT EUGENE RALPH spent the better part of his youth in Louisville, Kentucky, playing football and singing in punk rock bands. His work has appeared in several limited-edition chapbooks and in journals such as *Conduit*, *Mudfish*, *Exquisite Corpse*, and *The American Poetry Review*. He lives in rural western Kentucky, where he writes, teaches, and makes music with a revolving band of desperadoes and dreamers known as Brett Eugene Ralph's Kentucky Chrome Revue.

TOMAŽ ŠALAMUN lives in Ljubljana, Slovenia, and occasionally teaches Creative Writing at the American Universities. His last books translated into English are *Poker* (Ugly Duckling Presse, 2003), *Blackboards* (saturnaliabooks, 2004) and *The Book For My Brother* (Harcourt, 2006).

Fresh off the boat from Germany, BERND SAUERMANN was naturalized in 1971 and now resides in Cadiz, Kentucky. He is an associate professor teaching composition, literature, and film at Hopkinsville Community College. He received an MA in English Literature and an MFA in Creative Writing in 1993 from McNeese State University in Lake Charles, Louisiana. In 1983 he received a BS in cultural anthropology from Northern Arizona University.

BRENDA SHAUGHNESSY is the author of a book of poems, *Interior with Sudden Joy* (FSG, 1999). Her poems have been published in *Bomb*,

Boston Review, Conjunctions, The New Yorker, and elsewhere. She teaches at Columbia University and Lehman College and is the poetry editor at *Tin House*.

CHARLES SIMIC is a poet, essayist, and translator. He has published five books of essays, a memoir, numerous translations, and collections of poetry, the most recent of which is *My Noiseless Entourage* (2005). Among the many literary awards he has received are a MacArthur Fellowship and the Pulitzer Prize.

BRANDON SOM currently lives in Brooklyn. His poems have appeared or are forthcoming in journals such as *West Branch*, *Black Warrior Review*, *Good Foot*, and *Indiana Review*.

C.D. WRIGHT's most recent books are *Cooling Time: An American Poetry Vigil* (2005) and *One Big Self: Prisoners of Louisiana* (2002) with photographer Deborah Luster. She lives outside of Providence.

DEAN YOUNG's most recent book is *Elegy on Toy Piano* (Pittsburgh University Press, 2005). A new book, *embryoyo*, will be published by Believer Books later this year. He teaches at the Iowa Writers' Workshop.

PUBLICATION CREDITS

"Little Slave Narrative #1: Master" by Elizabeth Alexander. Reprinted from *American Sublime* (Graywolf Press, 2005).

"The Dream That I Told My Mother-in-Law" by Elizabeth Alexander. Reprinted from *American Sublime* (Graywolf Press, 2005).

"Nobody's Dead There" by Ralph Angel. Forthcoming in *Exceptions and Melancholies* (Sarabande Books, October 2006).

"The Heart of Things" by Ralph Angel. Forthcoming in *Exceptions and Melancholies* (Sarabande Books, October 2006).

"Stanzas before Time" by John Ashbery. Reprinted from *Your Name Here* (Farrar, Straus and Giroux, 2001).

"Of the 'East' River's Charm" by John Ashbery. Reprinted from *A Worldly Country: New Poems* (Ecco/HarperCollins, 2007).

"GONG" by Caroline Bergvall. Reprinted from *Fig* (Salt, 2005).

"Now II" by David Berman. Reprinted from *Actual Air* (Open City Books, 1999). Copyright 1999 by David Berman.

"The Charm of 5:30" by David Berman. Reprinted from *Actual Air* (Open City Books, 1999). Copyright 1999 by David Berman.

"Naming the Light" by Tina Chang. Reprinted from *Half-Lit Houses* (Four Way Books, 2004).

"six apologies, lord" by Olena Kalytiak Davis. Reprinted from *Shattered Sonnets, Love Cards, and Other Off and Back Handed Importunities* (Bloomsbury Tin House Books, 2003).

"Hair" by Mark Doty. Reprinted from *Turtle, Swan* (David R. Godine Publisher, 1987).

"Like God," by Lynn Emanuel. Reprinted from *Then, Suddenly—* (University of Pittsburgh Press, 1999).

"Twelve" by Forrest Hamer. Reprinted from *Middle Ear* (Roundhouse Press, 2000).

"The Blue Terrance" by Terrance Hayes. Reprinted from *Wind in a Box* (Penguin, 2006).

"Clouds Near San Leandro" by Brenda Hillman. Reprinted from *Pieces of Air in the Epic* (Wesleyan University Press, 2005).

"Wind Treaties" by Brenda Hillman. Reprinted from *Pieces of Air in the Epic* (Wesleyan University Press, 2005).

"Each Moment a White Bull Steps Shining into the World" by Jane Hirshfield. Reprinted from *The Lives of the Heart* (HarperCollins, 1997).

"Theology" by Jane Hirshfield. Reprinted from *After* (HarperCollins, 2006).

"Upon Waking" by Denis Johnson. Reprinted from *The Throne of the Third Heaven of the Nations Millennium General Assembly: Poems Collected and New* (HarperCollins, 1995).

"from" by A. Van Jordan. Reprinted from *M·A·C·N·O·L·I·A* (Norton, 2004). Copyright 2004 by A. Van Jordan. With permission of the publisher, W.W. Norton & Company, Inc.

"Disgraceland" by Mary Karr. Reprinted from *Sinners Welcome* (HarperCollins, 2006).

"Issues Involving Interpretation" by Ruth Ellen Kocher. First published in *Callaloo* 27.4 (fall 2004).

"Thanks" by Yusef Komunyakaa. Reprinted from *Pleasure Dome: New and Collected Poems* (Wesleyan University Press, 2004).

"Poem with the Morning Sun Reflected in Freshly Shined Shoes" by Gerry LaFemina. Reprinted from *The Window Facing Winter* (New Issues Poetry & Prose, 2004).

"Cheese Penguin" by Sarah Lindsay. Reprinted from *Primate Behavior* (Grove Press, 1997).

"Valhalla Burn Unit on the Moon Callisto" by Sarah Lindsay. First published in *Parnassus: Poetry in Review* 27.1-2 (2004).

"Land of the Discount Price, Home of the Brand Name" by Harryette Mullen. Reprinted from *Is This Forever, Or What?* ed. Naomi Shihab Nye

(Greenwillow, 2004).

"Sleeping with the Dictionary" by Harryette Mullen. Reprinted from *Sleeping with the Dictionary* (University of California Press, 2002).

"World's Bliss" by Alice Notley. Reprinted from *Waltzing Matilda* (Faux Press, 2002).

"Driving with Dominic in the Southern Province We See Hints of the Circus" by Michael Ondaatje. Reprinted from *Handwriting* (Alfred A. Knopf, 1999).

"Step" by Michael Ondaatje. Reprinted from *Handwriting* (Alfred A. Knopf, 1999).

"University Hospital Pathology Lab" by Heidi Johannesen Poon. First published in *Streetlight* 1 (spring 2002).

"The Anti-Leading Lady Dissociates" by Courtney Queeney. Forthcoming in *Filibuster to Delay a Kiss* (Random House, 2007).

"Eloping Alone" by Courtney Queeney. Reprinted from *Three New Poets* (Sheep Meadow Press, 2006).

"Picture" by Atsuro Riley. First published in *Poetry*, March 2004. Reprinted in *The Pushcart Prize XXX: Best of the Small Presses* (Pushcart, 2006).

"[untitled]" by Lisa Robertson. Reprinted from *Rousseau's Boat* (Nomados, 2004).

"My Frieze" by Lisa Robertson. Reprinted from *Debbie: An Epic* (New Star Books, 1997).

"A Common Sight" by Pattiann Rogers. Reprinted from *Firekeeper: Selected Poems, Revised and Expanded Edition* (Milkweed, 2005).

"In Addition to Faith, Hope and Charity" by Pattiann Rogers. Reprinted from *Firekeeper: Selected Poems, Revised and Expanded Edition* (Milkweed, 2005).

"Talking to Strangers" by Mary Ruefle. Reprinted from *Cold Pluto* (Carnegie Mellon University Press, 2001).

"Ideal Audience" by Kay Ryan. Reprinted from *The Niagara River* (Grove Press, 2005).

"Heated Passions" by Tomaz Salamun. Reprinted from *Blackboards* (Saturnalia Books, 2004). Translated from the Slovenian by Joshua Beckman and the author.

"Flor Ars Hippocratica" by Tomaz Salamun. Reprinted from *Poker* (Ugly Duckling Press, 2003). Translated from the Slovenian by Joshua Beckman and the author.

"prologue" by Kaia Sand. Reprinted from *interval* (Edge Books, 2004).

"the president probably talks" by Kaia Sand. First published on *Tinfish Net 2* (June 2005).

"Subtraction Forever" by Bernd Sauermann. First published in *Conduit* 8 (spring 2000).

"I'm Over the Moon" by Brenda Shaughnessy. First published in *BOMB Magazine* (fall 2005).

"That Little Something" by Charles Simic. First published in *American Scholar* 74.2 (spring 2005).

"The Devils" by Charles Simic. Reprinted from *Selected Early Poems* (George Braziller, 1983).

"Astral" by Tracy K. Smith. First published in *Callaloo* 28.4 (fall 2005).

"Duende" by Tracy K. Smith. First published in *Gulf Coast* 16.2 (summer/fall 2004).

"Leaving the Eccentric" by Larissa Szporluk. Reprinted from *Isolato* (University of Iowa Press, 2000).

"The Recluse" by Larissa Szporluk. First published in *Salt Hill Literary Journal* 15 (winter 2004).

"Distance from Loved Ones" by James Tate. Reprinted from *Distance from Loved Ones* (Wesleyan UP, 1990).

"The Radish" by James Tate. Reprinted from *Return to the City of the White Donkeys* (Ecco, 2005).

"Axionometric Manhattenings" by Rodrigo Toscano. First published as a broadside (Hive of One Press, 2003), designed and produced by Shanna Yarbrough.

"Simple Present" by Rodrigo Toscano. Reprinted from *Partisans* (O Books, 1999).

"Floating Trees" by C.D. Wright. Reprinted from *Steal Away: Selected and New Poems* (Copper Canyon Press, 2003).

"This Couple" by C.D. Wright. Reprinted from *Further Adventures With You* (Carnegie-Mellon University Press, 1986).

"How I Get My Ideas" by Dean Young. Reprinted from *Skid* (University of Pittsburgh Press, 2002).

"Rabbit, I Love You" by Dean Young. Reprinted from *Elegy on a Toy Piano* (University of Pittsburgh Press, 2005).